JDBBooklets Adv...

It's essential that you, the potential buyer, understand what Jdbbooklets is all about. This Advocacy (it supports a person or persons who publicly support or recommend a particular cause or policy) as a hobbyist writer fundraise for this charity by writing stories of different articles).

I am being specific; it is laid out importantly and concisely. Please note I am not a **Business; I** am a retired gentleman of 75 who is disabled with arthritis of the neck, spine, knees & feet, I also have Spinal Stenosis, and I wear a pacemaker. And I am classed as a **hobbyist author writer.**

My books are written; differently I tell the story with carefully written literacy and appropriate photographs from research. I spend seven days a week from 9 am to 5 pm researching and writing. Each book is written with understanding and contains fact, no fiction. Names are withheld unless specially allowed by newspaper research and author agreeance.

My plan is clear I will be selling my product to raise awareness of this terrible disease MNDA.

The other essential part of this hobby is the finance section. I do not make any money personally, except take back the exact amount incurred by postage, whether stamped by the Royal Mail or in Courier Format.

Receipts are issued in both cases and can be confirmed in writing and letter proof sent.

All profits go to MND by Bank Transfer, and MNDA will send me the monthly photographic proof of finances.

To be successful, I need you, the buyer, to understand why Funds are raised; I write to keep history alive the world over and locally and help others who have this dreadful disease of Motor Neurone. A condition that attacks the brain cells, nerves, and spinal cord and is a death sentence with no reprieve.

You can pay me directly D.Buettner- Banks Sort Code 20-30-81 A/C 63941175. Or you can pay via my paypal which is paypal.me/david72 or pay directly via my just giving crowdfunding page the link is https://www.justgiving.com/crowdfunding/jdbooklets

If JDBbooklets hasn't items readily available, he will re-order (but can only order in batches of 5). If you want more than one book, i.e. a business entrepreneur, please call direct, but I request that 15% of sales go to MNDA.

The books can be ordered from Fakenham Prepress Solutions, Unit 1. Marston & Langinger House 13 George Edwards Road, Fakenham NR21-8NL UK. Tel 01328-855783. www.fakprepress.co.uk.

Postage to the UK is based on weight and varies from £3.25 -£6.75 for each book.

Postage to international destinations again varies in post and weight of individual books, approximately £8.75 - £28 per book.

All books are placed carefully in white (A4-5). Envelopes with letters/receipts/invoices/compliment slips and placed and sealed carefully at no extra charge inappropriate padded envelopes (A4-A5).

If you wish the item to be tracked, this will incur extra expenses.

Jdbbooklets will store names individually with book ordered/date/time of postage and postal and courier price to avoid confusion.

Jdbbooklets entered a formal Fundraising agreement with MND on 1/03/20 signed with the Community Fundraiser Esther Fifield who can be contacted at Esther.fifield@mndassociation.org tel: 01604611867 MND Registered Charity No. 294354.

The Agreement states; All profits are made through the sale of JDBbooklets after postage. Timescale ongoing;

Jdbbooklets will not be held responsible for loss or damage in the postal system. Still, he will compensate with another book sent free (but postal charges will be paid by you, the purchaser) Jdbbooklets will have to see actual damage by photographs sent to david464u@icloud.com, then a new book will be posted Monday from Fakenham Post Office.

All books are registered with the UK Copyright Services Department, 4 Tavistock Avenue Didcot Oxfordshire OX11-8NA UK and jdbbooklets are allowed legally to implement the logo © on all his books & Website everything appertaining to JDBBooklets 1/3/20 to 1/3/25.

MNDA is registered with the Fundraising Regulator.

Thank You for your support and understanding, and in all my written books, I reserve the rights to © of my design and now ™ side of my logo.

I want to thank my Associate Designer Mr Tony Brooks who helped me with all my books, whether designing or altering items at my request; he has supported me from my first booklet 'Hands Across the Sea'.

My research material and photographs are fully acknowledged in the Bibliography section, legally credited.

I have raised a substantial amount thanks to you, the purchaser for MND.

I will continue as long as my health allows, but I will cease writing if I suffer further or my wife.

In the event of my death, any books written will end, and those held on file by Fakenham Prepress put on a stick and give back to my wife.

Fakenham Prepress must write to all those in my black address book informing them of my death; postage will be paid from our bank account, which will also be reported.

I want Adam of Fakenham Prepress to run the website three months after my death and close after that term with the wording of JDBBooklets closed.

My sincere thanks go to Manager Tristian Defew for standing by me since my writing and in the event of my death to inform the social media platform of my death and close JDBBooklets.

DavidBanks Author and Owner of JDBBooklets 22/11/20

This book we hope you find memories and more from the beautiful photos of our fair county to the magical and haunting stories of the past. Many books have been written about Norfolk but not in the manner of JDBBooklets.

The author isn't full time, he is a disabled hobbyist writer of 75 and because of such, all funds made by selling of books goes to his charity the MNDA. MNDA has given JDBBooklets their bank details and David has a contract with them as a full time representative. He has raised over £2610.00 since he began writing in MAY 2018.

Pay David direct for books to his Barclay account which is D. Buettner-Banks Sort Code 20-30-81 A/C 63941175 where he now transfers to the MNDA.

David works alongside his Associate Mr Tony Brooks who designs David's requests such as this beautiful cover and another Norfolk Memories Track of Time.

It is hard to believe David is 75 sadly disabled with arthritis and a pacemaker, but David's dedication shows no slowing up.

He has written a successful A5 Booklet of the London Underground called 'A Vintage Journey,' he has also written for a friend his Life Journey as a M/M on the Tube and he has written about a ship called 557/Lancastria which was sunk at St Nazarie June 17th 1940 with over 7,000 souls onboard. His next big book will be about the Moorgate Disaster with true Facts, as what he read a complete cover up.

David also hopes to write and complete a dedication to the 96BG USAAF who were based at Snetterton WW2 as the historian and well known and respected Geoff Ward suddenly passed away 15th November 2021

The photographer above is Malcolm Moulden who has allowed David to use his photographs as he is raising these funds for a charity who need help.

David thanks Tonys wife Tracey, and his own wife for being computer widows while these books are designed and printed.

Since starting my hobby it has grown, I spend nine hours a day, seven days a week on my computer writing stories, answering my mobile phone, sending emails to people and arranging office supplies and so much more. I don't charge for the envelopes only the post, everything else is with whom I've become, and my hobby has taken me all over the world. Research is astounding, people who help in my books, other authors now are aware whom Jdbbooklets is and his representation and assist, and eventually new script is written, read, and proofread.

I design all my covers and my associate Mr Tony Brooks assists too, and coming on board is a lady known as Vikki Bilbey a Copy & Content Writing Service Consultant.

JDBBooklets is growing and he hopes your,'' like the ever growing number of stories in his lovely written Norfolk books

He has his logo protected with the ™ mark and copyright on all his books as well as Tony in his designs. All JDBBoolets books are registered with the UK registration Service. Registration 284734963 & 284733035.

Other important information is that I have now signed on the 1/3/20 an agreement with MNDA and his point of contact is **Esther Fifield Community Fundraiser** and her email is **Esther.fifield@mndassociation.org her telephone is 01604611867.** I have the MNDA bank details if one would like to pay direct and the details are; Lloyds TSB, George Row, Northampton NN1-1DJ **Sort Code 30 96 09 A/C 02 95 26 79** quoting ref **RE 637606** The agreement also states all profits made through the Sale of jdbooks go to MND after postage is taken back, receipts of postage are held with Jdbbooklets..

Also Payment can be made direct to JDBBooklets by bank transfer and these details are such Pay D. Buettner- Banks Sort Code 20-30-81 A/C 63941175

My cheque to David Buettner Banks 9 st Peters road Walsingham Norfolk UK NR226DW

Or by paypal which is paypal.me/david72ok

Grab yourself a cup of tea and sit back and be transported back and experience a life you never knew by reading JDBBooklets on Norfolk.

LIMITED EDITION

No.

To.

Thank you for purcharshing this book, all proceeds go to M N D A less postage.

Norfolk Mardling

1.

Norfolk is a very pretty county, but to the visitor the names of villages is not pronounced as seen. First let's look at Hoverton, it's to locals spelt Hoffton, so on one's journey one is confused already, but thanks to joe-masons blog one will understand the terminology.

Puzzling is how to say Deopham (Deefham); Belaugh is perhaps not too mysterious (it certainly has nothing to do with laughter).

Tacolneston is another place that outwits those not in the know; for those people it is called Tackleston.

The town of Aylsham is pronounced Ellsham not Alesham by the locals Potterheigham on the River Thurne is known as potterham.

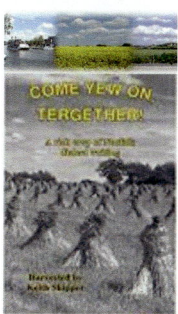

Places with Danish roots are quite common across Norfolk. The ending 'by' is frequently found. Thrigby is an example, but other areas of the county also exhibit Viking influence. Thorpe for instance is word with Danish roots. These placenames came about in the late ninth century and early tenth century when the Vikings ruled East Anglia. Then there is Swarffum or Swoffum = Swaffham; Deerum = Dereham; Dersnum = Dersingham.

Norfolk's relatively isolated location has meant that Norfolk dialect has survived, but with many others settling it is diminishing but by joining F.O.N.D. it, Can be kept alive.. 'Come yew together by Keith skipper has the perfect harmony of understanding, and like always the gentleman allows me to try to assist the furriners as locals say. Mardle magic is broad as its long but enjoy. It's as Keith says in his book it is impossible to convey the sound of Norfolk by means of a 26- letter alphabet.

From the huge volumes held by Eric Fowler of the EDP here is a sample to get your tounge's twisted.

Take for example a following remark made by a local when entering a public house with a empty pipe and pouch, he say 'Heya got inny bacci onya inna onya?, another a Norfolk man standing on a bridge as an express train thunders under ' She went shearing down the line, kicking up a dullor. She rushed inter har burrow, Lor, she shruck!'

A chuckle next adaptly named 'Grave laughter'. A story of Windum churchyard, an old man wot worked on a farm at Dykebeck uster take a short cut thru' the churchyard. The other chaps told him he'd be a seein' a ghost but he only larfed at em and kept a cumin' five the mornin' , summer, and winter. One of 'em thort he'd play a trick on him, so one mornin when he heered the old chap a comin' he hopped up onter a tombstone and started scrabblin away wi'his hands sayin', 'Lemmee git back, lemee git back!' The old man up wi' his stick and cracked him acrost the skull, sayin, 'Take that, you silly old b_, YOU SHOULDN'T HA' GOT OUT!.

The word 'wholly' is important in the Norfolk vocabulary, another word with meaning is 'Fare' and heard a bit is 'dorn't' We here in Norfolk do not tell you to your face that you are 'talking squit', we remark soon as you have gone with 'He/she dorn't know more about that than a crow do about a Sunday'.

But joining FOND you will still git to know the dialect better, or by Keith Skippers 'Larn yarself Norfolk. We tend to say 'bew'ul day not bootiful day, so our dialet is Squit: Talking nonsense, On the Huh: awry, slanted, Dwile: a course rag used as a floorcloth, Rum, curious, Dodman: garden Snail, Bor: neighbour, Mawther : young woman, Blah/Blar: to cry loudly, Fye Out: clean cut, Dickey: a donkey, Dickey: a donkey, Harnser, a heron, Ranny: any small object, On the sosh: Slanting, Trosh: to thresh,Trosel: threshold, Tittermatorter: see-saw, Plancer: a boarded floor, Swift: a newt, Nanny Dishwasher: a pied wagtail. So, put it All Togethers should sound like this? A short 'e' often becomes 'I', as in 'Git yew out o'the way' or ' I ent a ' gurn home, not yet I ent'. Then it can be transformed into a short 'u', as when 'shed' becomes 'shud'.

Norfolk is not simply a word that describes a county. "Norfolk" also describes a language, a humour, and a way of life. Spoken Norfolk has a stout and uniquely resistant quality and only people born in the county are able properly to penetrate it and repeat it with their own tongues. Just as their language, so also the people of Norfolk are tough, resistant and impenetrable.' 'For the traveller in search of the English Heritage, the county is a paradise. It has great cliffs and chalk downs, a history for older than any written documents, delightful rivers, unique still waters, low-lying fens, captivating towns, a historic roll of famous folk and a group of Saxon, Norman, and medieval churches crammed with beauty that makes England the matchless country in the world.'

The 29th September 1758 the dialect was started by this great man when he said "I am a Norfolk man, and glory in being so"; also said to Captain Hardy "Do you anchor" (an order, not a question, in the Dialect the man was Horatio Nelson .

Horatio Nelson was born on 29 September 1758, at a rectory in Burnham Thorpe, Norfolk, England; the sixth of eleven children of the Reverend Edmund Nelson and his wife Catherine Suckling. He was named "Horatio" after his godfather Horatio Walpole, 1st Earl of Orford (1723–1809),the first cousin of his maternal grandmother Anne Turner (1691–1768). Horatio Walpole was a nephew of Robert Walpole, 1st Earl of Orford, the de facto first Prime Minister of Great Britain. Nelson attended Paston Grammar School, North Walsham, until he was 12 years old, and attended King Edward VI's Grammar School in Norwich.

So full circle while less widely and purely spoken than in its heyday, the dialect and vocabulary can still be heard across the county, with some variations. It employs distinctively unique pronunciations, especially of vowels; and consistent grammatical forms that differ markedly from standard English. Its phrases are more in depth;

ar ya reet bor? (are you all right neighbour)

all of a muckwash (sweating profusely)

at that time of day (in those days, e.g., "beer only cost tuppence a pint at that time of day")

bred and born (used instead of "born and bred")

co ter heck (go to hell, an exclamation of amazement)

come on ter rain (starts to rain, as in "if that come on ter rain we shall get wet")

cor blarst me (oh blast me, when expressing, shock, surprise, or exasperation)

dew yar fa' ki' a dickir, bor? (Does your father keep a donkey, mate?) (See Dickir/ Dickie in vocabulary, below)

dew yews keep a troshin (means "carry on with the threshing" on its own but also means goodbye or "take care of yourself")

directly ("as soon as" or "immediately"), as in "Directly they got their money on Friday nights, the women would get the suits out of the pawn shop"

fare y'well (goodbye)

finish, at the/in the (eventually, as in "he gave it to her at the finish"; or "You might as well have went in the beginning, cause you had to go in the finish".)

fumble fisted (clumsy)

get on to someone (to tell someone off, as in "They all went quiet, but they never got onto father no more"

get wrong (told off)

getting again (born again pronounced gittin agin)

good on'yer (good for you or good of you) [this is also common in New England, an area that was originally settled by East Anglians]

he'll square yew up (he will chastise you)

The Fenians are coming (Phrase, typically referring to a commotion nearby. An old phrase originally referring to Irish travellers, who normally caused a commotion in towns they passed through)

he dint ortera dun it. (he ought not to have done it).

high learned (well-educated, clever)

hoddy-doddy (very small)

hold you hard ("hang on", or "wait a moment", from the practice of holding a horse's rein hard to stop it moving forward)

how much did you give for it? (How much did you pay for it?) [this is also common in New England, an area that was originally settled by East Anglians.]

I/we/you will hetter keep a dewun (no alternative but to keep going)

ill a bed an wus up (very sick)

lend us a lug (when asking someone else to listen in to a conversation for you)

let the dog see the rabbit (you're getting in the way, I can't see. dog pronounced dorg)

lolloping along (strolling along)

mind how you go (good-bye)

mobbed a rum'un (made a lot of fuss)

my heart alive! (expression of surprise, like "good gracious me!", sometimes shortened to "my heart" as in "my heart thas dear" meaning "good heavens, that's

expensive". When Norfolk people use the term "good gracious", they will sometimes say "good gracious on to me".)
over Will's mothers (black sky in any direction)
slummocking great mawther (fat girl)
suffun savidge ("something savage" - very angry)
thas a rummun (it's very strange)
that craze me! (that really annoys me)
war up (worn out)

My thanks to joe mason for starting these pages off, and to finish courtesy of William Dutt, about our wherry men's facts.

The story below true or false il I leave you to judge.
https://norfolktalesmyths.com/

"There wor a full mune, an' you could see th' mills an' mashes as clear as day. There worn't a breath of wind, not even enow to set th' reeds a-rustlin'; an' for over an hour arter sunset you couldn't hear a livin' thing a-movin' either by th' river or on th' mashes. I wor a-settin' in my cabin along wi' my mate Jimmy Steggles (him as used to hev th' owd Bittern), an' we wor a-talkin' about one thing an' another for a while afore turnin' in for th' night. All of a suddent we heered th' quarest kind o' screechin' a man ever heerd, an' lookin' out o' th' cabin I seed a man a-runnin' towards th' wherry as hard as he could put foot to th' ground. He soon got alongside on us, and I axed him what he wor a-screechi-n' about. `It worn't me, bor,' he say ; 'it wor suffin' what come outer th' shadder o' th' owd abbey. I wor a-goin' home to Ludham, arter lookin' arter some bullocks what are on a mash yonder, an' I thowt I heard suffin a-movin' about agin th' ruins." "Thinks I, that must be one o' them their cows what wor browt down here from Acle yesterday forenoon. So, I went outer my way a bit to see if anything wor amiss. When I got within about twenty yards o' th' walls suffin come a-wamblin' outer th' shadder o' th' owd mill,' (you know there wor a mill built on th' owd abbey years agone) ` an' started screechin' like a stuck pig. I never stopped to see what it wor, but jist come for yar wherry like hell in highlows ! ""He wor a chap I knew well-his father had an eel-sett up th' Thurne River-an' he wor a-tremblin' all over like a man wi' th' ayger. Both I an' my mate went ashore, an' I took my gun chance I'd wantin' it; but all we seed wor an owd harnsee (heron) go a-flappin' away acrost the mashes. An' it worn't a harnsee what made that screechin', I'll stake my life; though what it wor I never knowed. Whatever it wor it give that Ludham chap a funny fright, an' he wouldn't hear o' goin' home that night. So, we had to find a berth for him aboard th' wherry, an' he went on to Wroxham Bridge wi' us in th' mornin."

Was it the 'The Shrieking Monk' moans as he was being put on the makeshift gibbet made of a simple stout pole protruding out from the widow that faced a still misty river and marsh beyond? Then, no sooner had the noose been placed around the unfortunate's head, when he was pushed to swing in full view of those who had gathered below, and , tis always winter on dark nights between midnight and early dawn, particularly if the dawn is shrouded in a heavy mist and there is a distinct chill in the air, the story say It tells how this monk terrified a local wherryman one foggy night – All Hallows Eve and he rushes away to seek the safety of his wherry which is moored nearby; he slips in the early morning mud and falls into the Bure and is

drowned!, One thing is certain; all that is needed beyond these conditions is for a lone lapwing to swoop close by and send forth its pre-emptive cry of what might follow!

Manoeuvre your boat cautiously along the River Bure in early morning mist or will you walk the same path past the ruined Abbey,will you hear the plantiff cry,or the bell in the Abbey tower ring out eleven times, each ring echoing across the ladened empty marches. Was it happening ! are you witnessing? your near the gatehouse door; concerned are you with the apparitions? You hear the well lubricated bolts release the door ! What door their isnt but you hear it as plain as plain. Enjoy Your Holiday.

https://norfolktalesmyths.com/tag/shrieking-monk/

The End.

The Bull Inn

8 Common Place, Little Walsingham, NR22 6BP.

Enjoy good food, friendly landlord and great beer and a place to rest your weary limbs after sightseeing this beautiful village of ours rich in history. Yes Walsingham has it all. Walsingham is a civil parish in North Norfolk, England, famous for its religious shrines in honour of Mary, mother of Jesus. It also contains the ruins of two medieval monastic houses. Walsingham is 27 miles northwest of Norwich. Enjoy real ale, and pub grub, in a good ole Norfolk country pub. The Bull is a village institution, in the centre of the village in Common Place facing the Pump.

Telephone us on 01328 820333

Rivers of Norfolk & Historical Facts.

There are 40 different rivers in this fair county and in alphabetical order I have decided to write about a few of them so when next in this fair county maybe my investigation will show more when enjoying a cup of tea.

We start with the River Ainse (or Eyn) a small river in the county of Norfolk. It is a tributary of the River Wensum which it merges with at Lenwade The River Ainse has several tributaries also.

The watermill located on the river at Great Witchingham is known as Eade's Mill. Great Witchingham is a village and civil parish in the English county of Norfolk about 11 miles north-west of Norwich. The parish church of St Mary is a Grade I listed building dating from the 14th century. The Norfolk Wildlife Centre and Country Park, a local attraction also known as the Animal Ark, is in Fakenham Road.

Old Witchingham Hall, built in the 16th century, was demolished in the 1980s. It was once the home of John Norris (1734–77), High Sheriff of Norfolk for 1766. The village is also home too Great Witchingham Cricket Club, who play in the East Anglian Premier League.

The mill was built in 1666. Until 1948 the waterwheel was still in working order. By 1972 the watermill was still being used as a hammer mill to grind up pig meal and was powered by electricity. Today, the watermill and its surrounding buildings are listed.

Further travelling will being us to the River Ant is a tributary river of the River Bure in the county of Norfolk, England. It is (17 miles long and 8.75 miles are navigable) and has an overall drop of 27 metres from source to mouth.

It is said that the Ant was formerly known as the River Smale. The parish has a long history and was certainly long established by the time of the Norman Conquest, its population, land ownership and productive resources being detailed in the Domesday Book of 1086.

The river's source is just east of the village of Antingham in North Norfolk at Antingham Ponds.

Just below the pools the river's route has been used as a canal in the past, starting at what was Antingham bone mill. In 1812, as a wide gauge canal able to take a Norfolk wherry. The wherry "Ella" made the final trading journey on the canal from Bacton staithe in 1934. The river, now in its canal form, curves around the northeast of the town of North Walsham passing Bacton Wood Mill.

Below Bacton Mill the canal reaches a lock at Ebridge mill. At Honing Bridge, the course enters The Broads, administered by The Broads Authority. Here the canal cuts through a marshy wooded area called Dilham Broad and again curves to the east before resuming its southerly course to pass under Tonnage Bridge.

Below the bridge, it passes through Broad Fen, an area containing many drainage channels, and meets Tyler's Cut or Dilham Dyke, which runs off to the west.

It served the villages of Dilham and Smallburgh and was the furthest north that the River Ant could be navigated prior to the construction of the North Walsham and Dilham Canal.

During excavations for a new road in 1976, the remains of what was probably a Roman boat were discovered in the peat about 40 feet to the north-west of the bridge.

The work also discovered part of a wooden causeway, which ran from the site towards the ford which existed prior to the first bridge being built in 1797.

Just below the bridge, a wooden dug-out canoe was discovered during dredging operations on the river in 1927.

It was subsequently found to date from 720, and is the oldest boat found in Norfolk.

Continuing downstream the river passes the ruined remains of Moy's Drainage Mill, probably named after Percy Moy, who farmed land drained by the mill in the 1920s. The mill powered a single scoop wheel, which could also be driven by an auxiliary engine when there was no wind.

The river follows a straight course until it reaches Hunsett Drainage Mill. The structure

dates from 1860, and originally drove two scoop wheels to raise water into the river. The river turns to the south and passes a channel leading eastward to the staithes at Stalham and Sutton. As the river nears Barton Broad it passes a triangular island called The Heater. The channels either side lead to Barton Turf staithe. The river now enters Barton Broad, the second largest of the Broads, its size only exceeded by Hickling Broad.

It has a surface area of 170 acres and since 1995, much work has been carried out to increase the amount of open water and to dredge polluted mud from the bottom of the broad. Barton Broad is unique in that it has an island, called "Pleasure Hill.' It is believed that Lord Nelson learnt to sail on Barton Broad prior to joining the navy when he was aged 12.

Nelson was born into a moderately prosperous Norfolk family, Horatio Nelson was born on 29 September 1758 in a rectory in Burnham Thorpe, Norfolk. He was the sixth of eleven children of the Reverend Edmund Nelson and his wife Catherine Suckling. He was named "Horatio" after his godfather Horatio Walpole, 1st Earl of Orford (1723–1809). Nelson attended Paston Grammar School, North Walsham, until he was 12 years old, and attended King Edward VI's Grammar School in Norwich. His naval career began on 1 January 1771, when he reported to the third-rate HMS Reasonable as an ordinary seaman and coxswain shortly after reporting aboard, Nelson was appointed a midshipman and began officer training. Early in his service, Nelson discovered that he suffered from seasickness, a chronic complaint that dogged him for the rest of his life. Nelson rose rapidly through the ranks and served with leading naval commanders of the period before obtaining his own command at the age of 20 in 1778.

The Ant leaves Barton Broad at its southeast corner, at a point which is officially the normal tidal limit, it enters a stretch called "The Shoals" to the east of Irstead, a village with some fine thatched and half-timbered cottages.

The church building of St Michael is grade II* listed, and much of the fabric dates from the 14th and 15th centuries, although it was restored in 1839 and 1844. Like the cottages, it has a thatched roof. As the river meanders through the flat Broadland countryside, there are several drainage mills along its banks.

The first is Clayrack Drainage Mill, near to the entrance to Crome's Broad. This was moved here from Ranworth Marshes in 1981, as it was derelict and at risk of being lost forever.

It is one of only three hollow post windpumps in Norfolk and is maintained by the Norfolk Windmills Trust.

A little further downstream, also on the east bank is Boardman's Windmill. Boardman's drainage windmill was built in 1897 by a local millwright Daniel England of Ludham.

Trestle mills or Skeleton mills as they are sometimes described, were a later and less expensive alternative to a brick-built windmill. As a result of their mainly timber construction very few have survived the ravages of the weather and of time.

Boardman's mill is one of only three Trestle mills left on the Broads. Next the river passes How Hill nature reserve, which is open to the public. There are several nature trails, passing through sedge beds, marsh meadow and carr woodland.

Access is on foot, or in an electric boat. The site includes Toad Hole Cottage, a small marshman's house which was refurbished in the 1980s and is furnished to show what life was like in the 1880s.

How Hill staithe has a thatched boathouse, and the reeds which are cut for thatching are often stacked on the staithe to allow them to dry. Below How Hill the river makes a wide horseshoe bend, passing Neaves Drainage mill as it heads towards Ludham Bridge. The mill was built in 1870 but was becoming derelict in the 1970s. The wooden boat-shaped cap was replaced by an aluminium one in 2009, as the wood was rotten, and it lacks sails

Ludham Bridge drainage mill was built around 1877 but had lost its sails and fantail by 1934. During the Second World War it was used as a pillbox by the home guard.

Just the brick tower remains, and it has a distinctive lean to one side.

Ludham Bridge carries the A1062 road over the Ant. The tidal influence on the river at the bridge is about 7 inches .The river turns sharply east before straightening out a little. It then turns south and enters the river Bure at Ant Mouth. To the east of the junction are the remains of St James's Hospital. Chapel to Hospital of St. James, the last pilgrimage stops before St. Benet's Abbey.

We leave the River Ant on our tour of the rivers and historical facts and join The Babingley a minor river in the northwest of the county Norfolk in England.

It runs 12.2 miles from its source at the village of Flitcham to the River Great Ouse at Wootton Marshes where it terminates. In the hamlet of Babingley, near the river, Saint Felix of Burgundy is said to have landed c.630 AD to introduce Christianity to East Anglia. Local legend has it that St. Felix's ship was wrecked while travelling up the river Babingley. According to legend, he was rescued by beavers, and subsequently made a bishop.

The Babingley rises in "Further Back Wood," a little way east of the village of Flitcham, close to Abbey Farm. Its source is at a height of 82 ft. A watermill once stood on the riverbank, but traces of it are long gone; the watercourse and the millpond are all that remain.

The river runs through a gentle sloped valley westward and passes under the B1153 road and into Hillington Park.

There is tributary spring in a meadow on the Hillington side of Pond Farm, at Congham.

This tributary of the river is called the River Cong, flowing through the woods and over an impressive waterfall, where in the past it powered all the machinery within the Congham Oil Mill.

The mill is said to have been built for processing whales.

Whales were transported from King's Lynn docks by horse and wagon. The mill produced oil from whale blubber.

The resultant whale bones were then taken by road to Narborough Bone Mill where they were ground into fertiliser.

Some of the whale bones remain as ornaments at Congham Lodge to this day.

The waterfall that drove the mill remains.

There would have been a horrendous smell especially in the summer, which was why the mill was situated away from King's Lynn itself.

The Cong then flows on under the A148 and joins the Babingley close by the Gatton Waters caravan site.

After Hillington Park the river flows into the lake that served another long-gone watermill that stood close to Hillington Hall the now increased force of water once powered the large waterwheel at what, years ago was known as West Newton Paper Mill.

In the late 18th century sadly, the miller went mad, and his son then took over the business. It then changed over from making paper to grinding corn which lasted up until a few years after the last war.

From the lake the river runs through a wooded valley out of the Park and into the countryside south of the royal estate of Sandringham.

Sandringham House is a country house in the parish of Sandringham, Norfolk, England. It is the private home of Elizabeth II, whose father, George VI, and grandfather, George V, both died there. The site has been occupied since Elizabethan times, when a large manor house was constructed. This was replaced in 1771 by a Georgian mansion for the owners, the Hoste Henley's. In 1836 Sandringham was bought by John Motteux, a London merchant, who already owned property in Norfolk and Surrey. Motteux had no direct heir, and on his death in 1843, his entire estate was left to Charles Spencer Cowper, the son of Motteux's close friend Emily Temple, Viscountess Palmerston. Cowper sold the Norfolk and the Surrey estates and embarked on rebuilding at Sandringham. In 1862, William Cowper, later created Lord Mount Temple, sold Sandringham and just under 8,000 acres of land to Albert Edward, Prince of Wales, later King Edward VII, as a country home for him and his future wife, Princess Alexandra of Denmark. On the King's death, Sandringham passed to his daughter Elizabeth II. The Queen spends about two months each winter on the Sandringham Estate, including the anniversary of her father's death and of her own accession in early February. In the 1960s, plans were drawn up to demolish the house and replace it with a modern building, but these were not carried out. In 1977, for her Silver Jubilee, the Queen opened the house and grounds to the public for the first time.

We leave Sandringham and its rich history and journey finally on this little water course of time. The river now crosses into fen and marshland and passes under the disused railway bed of the line that runs from King's Lynn to Wolferton and once carried many members of the royal family on their way to Sandringham. The river now meanders in a northerly direction towards The Wash. It then switches into a man-made watercourse that directs it southward through Wootton Marsh towards Vinegar Middle where the river finally runs into the river Great Ouse estuary at Lynn Channel.

Coltishall was a place of note even when the Domesday Book was compiled. In 1231 the village was made a free town by King Henry III. For 250 years Coltishall was a centre of the malting industry. Many Norfolk wherries (trading ships) were built here. Wherry and Yacht Builder - Robert Collins who had learned his trade apprenticed to Samuel Press of Coltishall. The nearby RAF Coltishall played an important role during World War II, and afterwards, but was finally closed in December 2006. The site is now home to HMP Bure. John Alen, Archbishop of Dublin, was born in Coltishall in 14 on the bures journey we come to Belaugh St Peter a Church of England church located at the top of a steep slope above the village. It was built in the 14th century and contains an ornate rood screen decorated with images

of the apostles that appears to have been added in the early 16th century. In the 17th century a soldier loyal to Oliver Cromwell (described in a letter to Sheriff Tofts of Norwich as a 'godly trooper') scraped away the faces of the apostles, such images being regarded as idolatrous by many of Cromwell's followers. The church is supposed to be haunted Richard Slater - a servant at the village's rectory who stole money and jewels from the church and buried them in the rectory garden. When he later returned to dig up the stash, he was discovered by the rector. In the scuffle that followed, the thief drowned in the river. He is supposed to rise nightly to recover the money, only to be forced down again by the weight of the stolen loot. From 1330 Robert de Hurdeshulle and forty-nine other rectors to 1993 Andrew Parsons have served the church.

Leaving Belaugh our next port of the mighty bure is Wroxham. Wroxham Bridge was rebuilt in brick and stone in 1619 replacing a bridge built in 1576, which itself replaced an earlier, probably wooden, structure. It is the second most difficult on the Broads to

navigate (after Potter Heigham) and a pilot station sits on the Hoveton side of the river to assist boaters for a fee: £6 each way per boat.

On the northern side of the Bure is the village of Hoveton. Hoveton / is a village and civil parish in the English county of Norfolk. It is located within the Norfolk Broads, and immediately across the River Bure from the village of Wroxham. Hoveton has two churches, St Peter, and St John. Hoveton Old Hall dates from 1567 and features a Queen Anne style 17th century wing the originator of Hoveton Hall was Christabel Burroughes who commissioned Humphry Repton to construct the mansion in 1809.

Christabel was born in 1764. Her father was Henry Negus (1734-1807) a solicitor who worked in Bungay, Suffolk but who also owned Hoveton Hall. The Negus family had for a long time been wealthy landowners in the Hoveton area.

In 1789 Christabel married James Burkin Burroughes who had inherited Burlingham Hall in Norfolk (now demolished). The couple lived at Burlingham Hall for some time but unfortunately in 1803 at the age of only 43 James died leaving Christabel to care for seven sons and one daughter.

Now the area around Wroxham Bridge is a local shopping centre, mainly due to the presence of Roy's of Wroxham.

Roys was founded in 1895 when brothers Alfred and Arnold Roy opened their general store in the village of Coltishall.

The new store in Hoverton opened in 1899 was a mile down the road from the main Wroxham train station, all of Roy's supplies came by train, addressed to "Roy Brothers, LNER Station, Wroxham" and telegrams followed suit with a similar address. This was the beginning of the Roy's of Wroxham name.

World War I broke out in 1914 Arnold Roy was called up in 1916 and when discharged in 1921 his papers were signed by the then Secretary of State for War, Winston Churchill.

After the war, trade began to develop fast and the horse and cart delivery service covering the nearby villages was expanded with the purchase of a fleet of former Royal Mail Trojan delivery vans. These red vans set the corporate colours.

The company flourished, particularly in Wroxham where the company had expanded into tailoring, boots & shoes, drapery & millinery, pharmacy, ironmongery, furniture, carpets, and a motor garage. Roys even provided the street lighting and public lavatories. In 1931 the headquarters of the company was moved to Wroxham and the company Roy's (Wroxham) Ltd was formed.

Both Wroxham and Hoveton have several boat building and pleasure craft hire yards. John Loyne's started the first boat hire firm on the Broads at Wroxham where he moved the business, he had started in Norwich in 1878. Loyne's was obviously a shrewd businessman as, recognising the advantages of publicity, he took to making models of the boats he had for hire on the Broads and displayed them at exhibitions as an advertisement for his holidays.

Throughout the 1880's many other boatbuilders were following John Loyne's example and began to build and hire out cabin yachts.

However, his near neighbours the Collins family were time-served Master Wherry builders, and they had several Pleasure Wherries for hire. Plus, a good few more that were owned by other individuals but available for hire from Ernest Collins on a commission basis. The likes of these two famous businesses were very organised and actively involved in the holiday hire business. Several others amongst their contemporary companies would have for hire at least one pleasure wherry for the larger party. These included: Ernest Collin's brother Alfred who had the 'Rose' Ernest Collins was one of those entrusted with this service and in his list for 1908 he handled at least five such examples. Likewise, a few individuals might keep a wherry and hire it out for skippered cruises themselves. Several publicans did this including James Jimpson who

was the proprietor of the Kings Head Hotel (Hoveton) from 1865 - 1896. He kept the 'Enchantress .George Formby, the early twentieth-century entertainer, once owned a riverside home in Beech Road, off the Avenue, a thatched house called Heronby, built in 1907.

Further news April 2011 a base for the restoration of the Norfolk wherry was opened in Hartwell Road, by the Wherry Yacht Charter Charitable Trust Work began with the restoration of the Edwardian wherry yacht the Norada, with restoration of another wherry yacht, the Olive and the pleasure wherry, the Hathor, projected over the following two years. Once restored, the wherries are intended to be available for use by school and youth groups as well as by private charter. A third of the cost of the project came from the Heritage Lottery Fund. Leaving wroxham we journey on the Bure to:

Arthur Ransome's books Coot Club and The Big Six were written based on his time spent in Horning. Arthur Michell Ransome (18 January 1884 – 3 June 1967) was an English

author and journalist. Arthur was the eldest of four children: he had two sisters Cecily and Joyce, and a brother Geoffrey who was killed in the First World War in 1918.

Ransome's father was professor of history at Yorkshire College (now the University of Leeds).

 The family regularly holidayed at Nibthwaite in the Lake District, and he was carried up to the top of Coniston Old Man as an infant. His father's premature death in 1897 had a lasting effect on him. After a year at Yorkshire College, he abandoned his studies and went to London to become a writer.

His move to East Anglia brought a change of location for four of the books, Swallows and Amazons was so popular that it inspired several other authors to write in a similar vein.

Ransome died in a Greater Manchester hospital in 1967. He and his wife Evgenia are buried in the churchyard of St Paul's Church, Rusland, Cumbria, in the southern Lake District.

 Ransome won the inaugural Carnegie Medal from the Library Association, recognising Pigeon Post in the Swallows and Amazons series as the year's best children's book by a British subject.

His Swallows and Amazon books were "Swallows and Amazons series"
Swallows and Amazons (published 1930)
Swallowdale (1931)
Peter Duck (1932)

10.
Winter Holiday (1933)
Coot Club (1934)
Pigeon Post (1936)
We Didn't Mean to Go to Sea (1937)
Secret Water (1939)
The Big Six (1940)
Missee Lee (1941)
The Picts and the Martyrs: Or Not Welcome at All (1943)
Great Northern? (1947)
Coots in the North (unfinished) But he had a further twenty-three books from 1904.

Our next village on our journey to the sea is a quiet village approximately 9 miles from Great Yarmouth and 13 miles from Norwich Stokesby has the Ferry Inn, situated by the river's edge with limited moorings. Stokesby is part of the Flegg Hundred, which was an insular district in ancient times and in common with eleven of its neighbouring villages has the Danish termination 'by' to its name. 'Stok' was a word for outlying pasture near water where there was good grazing, and the cattle were kept during part of the year. Stokesby and its neighbour Herringby is listed in the Doomsday Book and at that time had a population of around 500 making them the largest village in Flegg. St Andrew's Church in Stokesby dates from the 13th Century. The Ferry House and Inn (now called The Ferry) with the lucrative 'Ferry' business and Staithe could afford their own large barn. There was money enough in the village to sustain a pork butcher and general shop. There was also a dressmaker, shoemakers, bricklayers, and a brazier. Flour was produced at the new windmill built-in 1827. A grand new Rectory was built in 1840 and a new school in 1876.
There was also a thriving Methodist congregation as well as a Wesleyan Chapel.
There is a memorial plaque in the Church listing the 65 Stokesby men who fought in the Great War, a staggering percentage of the adult male population at that time.

Now journeys end Great Yarmouth. Great Yarmouth (Gernemwa, Yernemuth) lies near the site of the Roman fort camp of Gariannonum at the mouth of the River Yare. Its situation having attracted fishermen from the Cinque Ports, a permanent settlement was made. and the town numbered 70 burgesses before the Norman Conquest. Henry, I placed it under the rule of a reeve. Yarmouth is an antient town, much older than Norwich; and at present, though' not standing on so much ground, yet better built; much more complete; for number of inhabitants, not much inferior; and for wealth, trade, and advantage of its situation, infinitely superior to Norwich. In 1797, during the French Revolutionary Wars, the town was the main supply base for the North Sea Fleet. In 1724, Defoe visited Yarmouth as part of his Tour Through the Whole Island of Great Britain and was very impressed by what he saw. He was quick to appreciate the town's geographical location and how it controlled Norwich's access to the North Sea. The town was the site of a bridge disaster and drowning tragedy on 2 May 1845, when a suspension bridge crowded with children collapsed under the weight killing 79. They had gathered to watch a clown in a barrel being pulled by geese down the river. As he passed under the bridge the weight shifted, causing the chains on the south side to snap, tipping over the bridge deck. Charles Dickens visited Great Yarmouth in 1849 - staying at the Royal Hotel on Waterloo Road.

Anna Sewell - the authoress of Black Beauty - was born in Great Yarmouth However, she didn't write the book until she was 57 years old and living in Old Catton near Norwich. She only wrote one book during her lifetime, but it has remained a children's classic ever since. The house is now used as a restaurant. Anna Sewell died shortly after Black Beauty was published and she was buried in the graveyard of the Quaker Chapel at Lamas.

The Tollhouse with dungeons, dating from the late 13th century, is one of Britain's oldest former gaols and oldest civic buildings. It backs onto the central library. Major sections of the medieval town walls survive around the parish cemetery and in parts of the old town.

Great Yarmouth railway station is the terminus of the Wherry Lines from Norwich. Before the Beeching Axe, the town had several stations and a direct link to London down the east coast. The only remaining signs of these is a coach park, where Beach Station once was, and the A12 relief road, which follows the route of the railway down into the embankment from Breydon Bridge.

The Lydia Eva, the last surviving steam drifter of the Great Yarmouth herring fishing fleet. The Great Yarmouth herring fleet had made the town the major herring port in the world in the early part of the 20th century. The Lydia Eva general statics are Class and type: Sidewinder trawler

Tonnage: 138 grt 64 net
Length: 95 ft
Beam: 20.6 ft
Depth: 9.8 ft
Installed power:
Engine: 1930, Crabtree & Co. (R.H. Hutchinson), Triple Expansion, 10" + 17" + 28" x 20".
Boiler: 1961, Stockton Chemical Engineers & Riley Boilers Ltd., RT Scotch.
The National Historic Fleet is a list of historic ships and vessels located in the United Kingdom, under the National Historic Ships register. National Historic Ships UK is an advisory body which advises the Secretary of State for Culture, Media and Sport and other public bodies on ship preservation and funding priorities.

So, the mighty Bure comes to the North Sea and our journey ends.

THE END

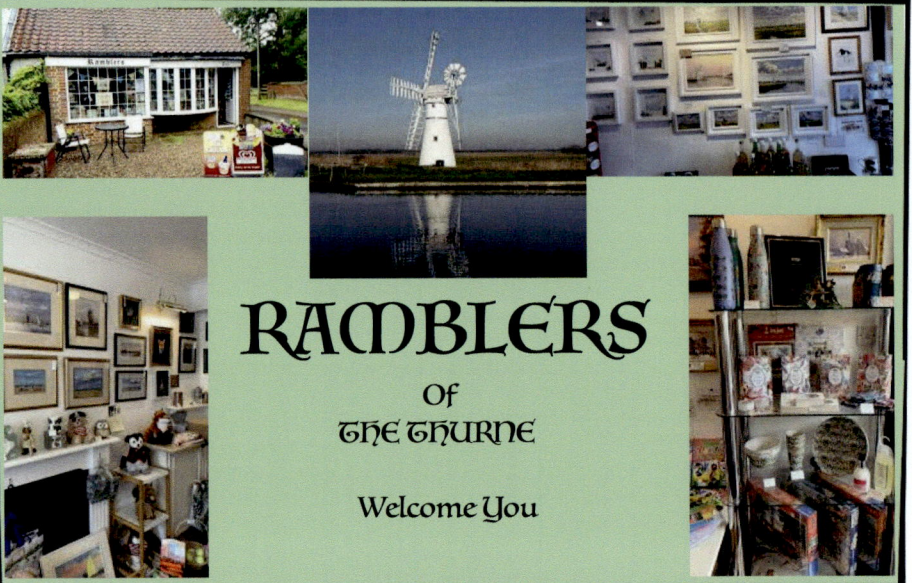

RAMBLERS

Of
THE THURNE

Welcome You

Beautiful range of paintings in stock, along with a special selection of gifts and locally produced tasty treats.

Hot drinks and grocery items, as well as superb local ice cream and Apple Juice.

Also we have David Blakes books including his latest offering the 'Wherryman'.

Plus books from the disabled author David Banks AKA Jdbbooklets.

Signed copies of Chris Crowthers 'The Water Shed'.

Hope to see you soon

Opening Easter & **hours will be** <u>**9am-5pm**</u> **7 days** a week

We Close the end of October

Memories of Great Yarmouth
1.

Sometimes in our lives, we have visited Great Yarmouth where the Sea life shaped East Anglia as we know it forward on many years and it was a hive of activity and brought people together from homes, and factories, it was a seaside town of plenty, and it brought many memories.

Childhood and teenage years memories of Great Yarmouth, the packed sea front in summer with all its many amusement arcades and attractions the equally packed Regent Road ...?

Can you remember perhaps some mornings or an afternoon boarding The Golden Galleon which would set off from the Haven Bridge for a trip on the Norfolk Broads?

Childhood memory as to when the Scottish boats & families came down each year from Peterhead, Aberdeen and Fraserburgh for the herring fishing season, anyone remember those days!

Or your taste of caravan life, adventure at South Denes Caravan Park; there was never

any question of it being anywhere else.

From Trevor Bradshaw I spent many happy holidays there in the early 1950's used to hire a caravan from "skippers caravans" right on the sea front. They were all named with names like Sunny Morn, Breezy Morn, etc. I can vividly recall the year 1951 when the power station was being built, and they were pile driving for the water outlet into the sea and the chimney was under construction.

From a gentleman now living in Australia named Gary Cooke, he say's 'It was our annual holiday site every summer. We used to stay in a caravan just down from the "big" funfair. I remember the gas lights in the caravan and changing the mantels when they broke.

but if one walks from South Denes only ghosts of yesteryear, nor lovely caravans, everything shut and falling to pieces, but such lovely memories! the laughter of ghosts long ago can be heard, wondrous excitement of the little children, now adults bringing perhaps their children to Great Yarmouth and telling them the golden days of happiness and plenty, days that started for many like;

Each day mum would give us all a bag of 1 penny and 2 pence pieces to last the day and they almost always did . We used to go the arcade and play on the horse's race game and how sad it is, but my favourite thing was a machine with a chicken in and it clucked as it dropped an egg with a toy inside.

A story from a lady born and bred in Great Yarmouth buying chips on the market on the way home to dinner (I live down Newtown) 4 pence!! Bus fare tuppence I think.

Marching over to Cobholm for our game's lessons in the summer, weekly swimming lessons in the old swimming pool, freezing! I was always bringing a note with some excuse not to attend.

The holiday well and truly started as one family recalls approaching Great Yarmouth from "The Acle straight". The horizon always revealed outlines of familiar places long before we had arrived; the chimney from the power station on South Denes, Nelson's monument and as we drew closer even the top of the big dipper at the Pleasure Beach would become visible.

 Driving along the seafront towards South Denes, one's head would be hanging out of the window getting the first lungful of sea air so fresh from the London Smog.

Yarmouth sea air-cured all ills, once we had arrived at the site and collected the keys for the caravan from the camp office, we would go straight to the caravan - which was always on the front row. It was wonderful the feeling of freedom in our metal home all cleanly laid out, and after unpacking the car, lunch would be served miraculously produced on the tiny cooker in the van, but it was beautiful.

Breakfasts in the little caravan smelt wonderful, the bacon sizzling, and the aroma filled our home on two wheels.

After breakfast, it would be off to the toilet blocks with your toilet bag under your arm and a towel over your shoulder to get a wash and to clean your teeth. The washbasins had "push button" taps on them; you had to push them down hard and as soon as you took your hand off it the tap would slow to a trickle and then stop, too hard and one would get drenched, and laughter could be heard.

When we used to go out one favourite to watch was the Guinness Clock on the front, at some time while we were out, the sea air also brought hunger pains and the cockles, mussels, and whelks were always close by.

The beaches were always packed with holidaymakers: building sandcastles, swimming in the sea and lounging on deckchairs enjoying the sunshine.

They came in by trains or coaches, the local hotels bursting, Summer holidays seemed long and sunny, and they were "free" We had jam sandwiches and lemonade made from crystals with water and shaken in the bottle.

It was bliss, so many people all enjoying this designated holiday spot. I was born 1950 and at the age of 10 years I started to earn a livening with my Barrow that my father (Tosh) had made from old wood and pram wheels.

We lived on Audley St right next to Beach Coach Station as it was Beach Station and going through my childhood I remembered the Steam Trains and their whistles and smoke rising from the platform roof.

From a Mr Howard word would be said : Beach Coach Station, that's the place, Full of people, cars, and haste, "A barrow for your luggage sir" Blanking moments-they confer. Then, on the barrow, the luggage goes, Overloaded, and it shows, Give the customer a smile, The destination - half a mile.

VISIT EAST ANGLIA'S PREMIER AMUSEMENT PARK!!

THE PLEASURE BEACH

GREAT YARMOUTH

OPENING FOR THE EASTER HOLIDAY AND EVERY WEEKEND UNTIL WHITSUN THEN OPEN DAILY FROM 10 a.m. SUNDAYS 2 p.m.

THRILLS!!!

THE WORLD'S LARGEST ROLLER COASTER

SUPER GO-KART TRACK

Exciting New Alpine Chair Lift

LAUGHS & THRILLS FOR YOUNG & OLD

RAIN OR SHINE THE PLEASURE BEACH IS FINE

UNDER THE PERSONAL DIRECTION & SUPERVISION of **BOTTON BROS.** AMUSEMENTS LIMITED

OUR BUSINESS IS YOUR PLEASURE

The Barrow boys came from all parts of the town, and we got to be friends and rivals with each other.

But when we had problems with the taxi drivers we would all stick to together , as they didn't like us nicking their trade. I used to earn quite a lot as I was on the scene early about 6am and carried on all day till about 5pm. During this period, I would nip indoors for a bite to eat and drink being close by, and this would save me money on food, but I always had my sweets.

The ever exciting 'Pleasure Beach' with it's wonderful and unique landmark 125ft tall double Ferris wheel (see Yarmouth from the air!), golden gallopers, jets, waltzer, satellite, ghost train, fun house, helter skelter and

of course the giant slide and ancient roller coaster! 'Free rides' night just before Easter opening was a highlight of a Yarmouth child's year. Local Lad Colin Browne says "As a young boy growing up in the 40s & 50s I explored the length and breadth of the whole of our town, so many friends not so many enemies.

Karl Kay says "I was 8 years old then, the height of my pedal car career). My grandparents took me to Gt. Yarmouth from the mid 60's up until 1975. They had holidayed there with my mother prior to this.

We started at the Vauxhall Camp site, progressing to guest houses by the early 70's.

There were, at one time, two boating lakes on the 'Golden Mile'. The Northern one, next to the Waterways, is still going strong, probably because of its proximity to the Waterways, which itself has now faded into the background.

The Southern one, which was adjacent to the Pleasure Beach, has long since vanished into history, becoming part of the Log Flume ride.

Whilst people enjoyed holidays, work in the town had to carry on and one famous

factory that has since sadly gone is "Birds Eye. 'The men worked 12 hours Monday to Saturday and either 8 or 16 hours on a Sunday to affect a shift change between days and nights, i.e., either 80 or 88 hours a week.

One lady recall working at Birdseye, Jan 1956 just after I was married. I started on the fish fingers conveyor belt, then went on to the end of the belt on the packing machine.

Also noted by another worker, it was rather interesting when the foil containers stuck to the belt rather than slide into the box the machine had so precisely assembled resulting in a crushed foil container and razor-thin slices of beef and sticky gravy all over the machine.

Quality Control says interestingly "Before 1960 harvesting, threshing, and vining of peas was carried out in the field and vined peas were tested with tender meters at several locations.

From 1960 peas were harvested and brought for threshing and vining to two large stations at Filby and Upton. Each batch of vined peas was tested with a tender meter and graded 1 to 6. Periodically tender meters were checked against control samples provided by Unilever's Research Establishment at Colworth House in Bedfordshire.

The intention was that peas would be processed, frozen and placed in cold storage within 90 minutes of vining. Another worker stated; My main concern was the awful overalls and hairnets we had to wear.

I was very young and fashion-conscious then!

I started off packing beef burgers of the conveyer belt into boxes.

You had to be very fast, or the beef-burgers would be coming at you from everywhere!

The new shift was meant to be in place before the old shift finished, so the conveyer belt never stopped. If someone went off before the new shift had got in their place there would be a MOUNTAIN of burgers to sort out! The only time it stopped was when the box machine got jammed up.

"Birdseye paid the best wages that you could find in the town. I was 18 by then and was probably one of my last summer jobs in Great Yarmouth and we were on 12-hour shifts from 6 in the morning to 6 p.m. or 6 p.m. to 6 in the morning so you had to alternate. The wages were 2 shillings to 2/6 for 12 hours; that's 25 bob a day.

Now if the peas were not tender enough, because this is Birds Eye, remember, and the adverts on television fresh as the time when the peas went pop, it was my job to test the peas.

From the factory floor to the young lasses that had the cold and smelliest job in Great Yarmouth the that they could process the catch as soon as it came off the boats the humble herring - known as the silver darlings - that the town of Yarmouth owes its origin and much of its subsequent prosperity. One person who wishes to remain obnoxious says I would like to share that when a young lad, I and my younger brother would play truancy from school spending most of our

time and days between the palladium and the quay usually nicking a herring or two to take home for tea. These little smelly darlings were well sought after! And the Scotch girls who did much of the processing of the catch on the quayside, needed lodgings!

So, to the guest houses which were in demand by the holidaymakers, and the Scottish girls, one such comment came forth with owners of a guest house. We first started running the Winchester guesthouse in 1951, most people came from the Midlands, at that time we used to have three meals a day, breakfast 8.30, dinner 1.00 and high tea at 5.15. For breakfast, you'd have cereal and bacon and egg. For lunch you'd have three courses, soup to start with, main course and dessert and coffee if they wanted it. High tea was a salad or sometimes smoked haddock or pie and chips.

We used to get up about 6.00 in the morning to get the water on and the breakfast cooked, because we used to take in 42 people and we only had 2 bathrooms for them all, they had to manage like that. We had hot and cold running water in each room. The guests used to come down at 8.30am and everybody was served together. Then we'd prepare dinner. Then in the afternoon, we had to get the salads ready for the evening meal. Then after that get ready for breakfast in the morning again. We were working all day 7 days a week.

Another guesthouses daughter stated 'My mother ran a boarding house, and our lives were run to the season. After January, Mother went into a frenzy of cleaning and decorating ready for Easter. Sometimes we had a casual visitor. Mother had her regulars of commercial travellers. The big start was Whitsun (six weeks after Easter).

We had Bed & Breakfast people, Full Board which usually meant three meals and a light supper, and apartments when visitors hired rooms and provided their food for Mother to cook.

These were cleaned and jugs filled twice a day a goe's under was provided too, as the toilet was in the back yard.

The men usually came down for hot water to shave and the family to wash with.

We all had to help and learned at an early age Mother's Way was the only way and God helps you if you didn't do it right. Featherbeds were the order of the day, which had to be shaken and turned every day. The rooms were swept, using a scattering of cold tea leaves - it helped to draw the sand together. Mats were taken outside and shaken; skirting boards and even the springs under the bed were dusted.

After I'd finished, Mother would inspect - if there was a small amount of dust on her finger, I had to do it all again with her watching.

I lived at 3 Eagleton Villas from about 1950 - 1955. My grandparents lived next door from which they ran a small hotel. We accommodated the 'overspill' during the busy summer months. I remember having to move into the attic when the hotel was full from where could see the bus/coach station. I would watch for my dad, who was a football referee, coming back from a match on a Saturday. Although I was very young I still have fond memories of Great Yarmouth! There was no plumbing in the bedrooms and washstands with a marble top and splashback with a pewter jug full of cold water and slop pail underneath provided washing facilities. Behind Woolworth's on the Quay was the Slipper Baths, I think this would be where people that did not have baths in their houses would go for a bath. I remember there was like a path like a maze

Transport for many wasn't a car, but by train or bus, or coach, humour played an important role if, and many times it was heard that holidaymakers leave their brains at home when they go to the seaside. The bus may have announced "The Beach" in big letters at the front and the back and even at the side but it was still necessary to ask of the driver or the conductor, "Does this bus go to the beach". To help nonlocals Some of the old buses had a moving screen behind the driver's seat that showed advertisements for local shops and events. The Blue Buses also ran to Caister though they were single decker's. The Easton County's Buses were red, and they set of from near the Bath Hotel running to Lowestoft.

From Buses to Port authority posts and workers, Great Yarmouth was never still.

One gentleman recalls; My father was a stevedore down at the docks, he was employed on a casual basis in the fishing season from September to December. Usually, he would queue each day as the ships came in and allocated to a job by the gangmaster who would say how many men were needed for the day.

German air raids targeted Great Yarmouth for the first time in summer 1940. Most

bombing raids on the town occurred in 1941. 800 high explosive bombs were dropped that year. One can remember the air raids and the sirens and having to spend cold nights down in the Anderson shelter in our small front garden. Many streets had bombed buildings, sometimes rows of them. Inside walls were now outside. Fireplaces & chimneys, stairways leading to nowhere. There were no fences around them.

One home had the double sliding doors blown off, Bombed ruins were playgrounds in the 1940s and '50s.

New streets were forming from the bombed areas, and people who had lost their homes were rehoused in these new prefabricated buildings. Prefabs (short for 'prefabricated' houses) were built out of necessity after the Second World War as relief

housing, as they were very quick and easy to erect, being made from prefabricated concrete and asbestos sections, and were relatively cheap to build. In a gale the pre-fab's roof used to bang up and down and was full of asbestos. Did not harm us or our kids. We enjoyed the indoor toilet and a nice bathroom. We may well look back on the pre-fabs with a bit of amusement, distain, or disbelief now, but at the time most people seemed impressed with their 'modishness'

Yarmouth was changing, but people had to be housed. Yet amazingly the Rows seemed to stay intact Nobody knows for certain how or why the Rows originated as a distinctive town layout system, perhaps unique to Great Yarmouth. They appear to go back to the 11th century when the sandbanks at the mouth on the River Yare were first settled as a recognisable community of fishermen. The Rows were identified by traditional names, though they were not numbered until 1804, when there were 145. Perhaps the best known was Kittiwitches Row (no. 95) which was also the narrowest, being just 30 ins. at its western end. This may originally have gained its name from Kit Witchingham, a 17th century baker who lived here, though there are many other theories about witches and strange happenings in this row. The Rows were extremely narrow, mostly too narrow for a normal horse cart to pass down. (The solution to this was the 'Troll cart', which was specially constructed to be narrow enough to pass through most of the rows, and after which the 'Troll cart.

Events happening in Great Yarmouth which affected all of Norfolk was the 1953 floods, losing one's home in the second world war was one thing, but 7 years later a high tide and the wind is in that quarter, Residents, were well-used to battering's from the elements, had spent the afternoon preparing for a 'normal' storm as best they could, securing their boats, shoring up shrubs and trees, and generally battening everything down in readiness for a wild night, but this storm was to have terrible consequences for many.

Great Yarmouth and Lowestoft were the next towns of any size to be hit twice in the case of Great Yarmouth, as the banks of the five-mile-long Breydon Water to its west gave way, so that water flooded into the town from its rear shortly after the sea had battered it from the front.

9 people died and around 10, 000 had to be evacuated.

It was a dreadful It quite unbelievable, people were amazed to hear the news and the extent of the flooding; never dreaming it could be so widespread and devastating.

One person remembers 31 1 1953 as usual I was going roller skating in the winter gardens on arrival we were told due to high winds the glass in building was unsafe so we made our way to the empire cinema during the film a message came on the screen for anyone living in Cobholm and Southtown to go home at once no reason was given but when the film was over a message was shown telling everyone to leave the cinema by the side exit doors on leaving we walked to front of the cinema to find the sea lapping the front steps when I got home to havelock road the water was all over the road but not in the house my father was a coach driver for Norfolk motor services and he had parked his Bedford coach in Clarence road outside Richmond & Pritchard's garage and all you could see was the coach roof.

Another gentleman remembers and says I can remember the flood of 53. I would be about 5 at the time. We lived on Jellicoe Rd ;my father was a policeman. I can remember him coming home soaking wet ,he took off his wellington boots and water came out of them over the kitchen floor. We didn't see much of him over the next few days ,only to change into dry clothing and go back on duty, I can remember my mother taking me over Jellicoe bridge to the sea wall and looking at the water lapping up the wall. It would have been a few hundred yards normally to the sea. We were luckier than a lot of people, especially those in Cobham and Southtown

When the dawn came on Sunday, the east coast of England was an appalling sight: The monstrous surge in the night had made nonsense of the maps, Great Yarmouth and its land was unrecognisable from the air. At the Quayside Woodblock, surface of the South Quay broken up by the storms.

Sea Palling

To summarise the night of 1953 a young resident of Yarmouth at the time said I believe the sea came in as far as Stalham. Several people in the same family died in the pub at the gap at Sea Palling.

From the storms to our memories of Great Yarmouth, I wonder how many readers will say "I remember that?"

Great Yarmouth had five theatres, which would all have live shows during the summer season.

The theatres were the: Wellington Pier, Britannia Pier, The Windmill, The Aquarium (now the Hollywood cinema) and the ABC (this was where Clinton Cards and Pizza Hut are now).

Artists playing at these venues like Joe Brown, Billy Fury, Tommy Steele, Ronnie Ronald, Mike and Bernie Winters, Cannon and Ball and many more.

Woolworth's was on Regent Road, and everything cost less than sixpence. Old money!

You could go on boat trips out to Scroby Sands to see the seals; these went from the beach and somewhere

As the writer I can remember the Market place, but we are entering the realms of the late 80s, one such stall always had many people talking, but equally many people spending, it was 'Barrie's Bacon Rolls' they were simply delicious, you could see the bacon cooking, and the cuppa to wash it down must be one of the best I've tasted, made with tea-leaves. Went with my late neighbour Mr Derek Reynolds of initially Ludham then Horning.

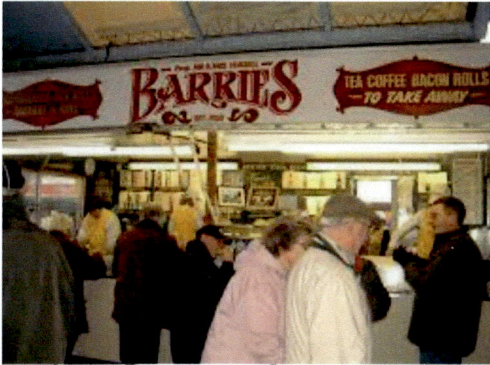

His assistants always topping kettle with water, sadly I was told Barry passed away and I have moved on but have many happy memories of Great Yarmouth.

The shops down Regent Road (how it used to be) full of goodies, everything changing, memories linger.

I would love to hear of your stories, what do you remember!?

THE END

JANUARY.

"The Duke of Grafton's hounds unkenneled a fox at Fakenham Wood, near Euston, and after a chase of upwards of 50 miles in 4 hours 5 minutes, killed him at New Buckenham."

MARCH.

A mob assembled at Lynn and grossly assaulted several millers and farmers by throwing at them stones and dirt. In the evening they broke the windows in the dining-room of the Duke's Head Inn. "One of the ringleaders was taken to gaol, and by the active exertions of the Rutland Militia tranquillity was restored without bloodshed."

The remains of Miss Sophia Goddard, of the Theatre Royal, Norwich, were interred at St. Peter Mancroft. Mr. Hindes, the manager, and the principal actors attended on the melancholy occasion. This young lady had obtained considerable reputation on the Norwich boards, and was making rapid advance to eminence in her profession when death prematurely deprived the theatrical world of an actress whose talents would have ensured her success on any stage. She supported with great fortitude and resignation a long and painful illness, brought on by exertions that her constitution was unequal to, and died on Sunday last (March 15), in her 26th year, sincerely beloved and lamented by her family and friends."

In March the British Fleet gathered in Yarmouth Roads. Nelson joined the Fleet at Yarmouth and sailed to the Baltic, winning the Battle of Copenhagen

APRIL.

John Allen (23) and John Day (26), for burglary at the house of the Rev. Isaac Horsley, at North Walsham; Richard Grafton, for stealing a cow and three heifers; and James Chettleburgh (36), for stealing six sheep at Saxlingham, were executed at Thetford. "Day confessed to having committed four burglaries previous to that for which he suffered, and to having deserted thirteen times from different regiments."

JUNE.

The body of William Suffolk, who was executed in March, 1797, for the murder of Mary Beck, of North Walsham, was taken down by authority of the magistrates and interred on the spot where the gibbet was erected. "About ten days back a starling's nest, with young ones, was taken out of the breast of Watson, who hangs on a gibbet on Bradenham Common, near Swaffham, for the murder of his wife, which was witnessed by hundreds of people as something very singular and extraordinary.

Holkham Sheep Shearing commenced and lasted until the 26th. Among those present were the Duke of Bedford, the Duke of Manchester, and other distinguished visitors.

The new implements exhibited included a machine for drilling turnips, invented by the Rev. T. C. Munnings. It was described as "nothing more than a perforated tin box, affixed to and vertical with the axis of a wheelbarrow." A thrashing machine "was much approved of." At this meeting Mr. Coke announced his intention to give premiums for promoting the improvement of live stock and for encouraging experimental husbandry.

Letter from Mr. Thos, Everett, Wiafarthiog Norfolk, dated June 1801. Mr. Woodcock, — Dear Sir, I he? to add my testimony to the efficacy of Pack Woodcock's Wikd Pills. My wife had been aldicted for about twenty years with min in the stomach and hotly ; the violent WlchinjM or wind were dreadful that she might be heard all over the house, and indeed her life was almost misery to her, the pain Ixdug great and so frequent. She has sometimes quite wished for death to put end to her sufferings. On. three occasions after violent snasms in the stomach, sho vomited great deal of blood, at one time from three to four pints. She applied to various medical men, but to no purpose, they did her no good. Seeing one of your advertisements I resolved to get her to try your celebrated "WIND PILLS." After the first dose she obtained comfortable night's rest and gradually got better, and is now* quite vrlf. She has had no return of the bleeding, and does not suffer with wind, and eats two three times much she did before. Wishing you every success with these valuable Pills, I remain, dear Sir, yours truly, THOMAS EVERETT. Witness to the correctness this letter, T. W, Smith.I Sufferers from WIND IN THE STOMACH, INDIGESTION.

A fire broke out on the roof of Norwich Cathedral, and occasioned damage to the amount of £500. Bishop Manners Sutton personally distributed refreshments to the soldiers and others who assisted in extinguishing the flames. About 45 feet of the roof were destroyed. The fire originated from the carelessness of plumbers at work upon the building.

JULY.

Wroxham Regatta took place. "The novelty of a sailing match attracted a great deal of company." It was won by the Union, the property of the Rev. Mr. Preston.

AUGUST.

The annual Venison Feast was held at the Red Lion, Fakenham, to celebrate Lord Nelson's victory of the Nile.

SEPTEMBER.

A person residing in this city has within the last week been convicted in penalties amounting to £166 10s., for having laid a leaden pipe from his dwelling-house to communicate with the pipes belonging to the proprietors of the waterworks, without having obtained their consent or paid the accustomed water rent. The amount was paid to the company's solicitor, who immediately returned the money, except 30 guineas, which he has paid to the Norfolk and Norwich Hospital for the benefit of that institution

OCTOBER.

At Yarmouth, during the Peace illuminations, a mob broke the windows of several houses occupied by Quakers. The ringleaders were committed for trial at the Sessions.

NOVEMBER

Peter Donahue, a sergeant in the 30th Regiment of Foot, was executed at Lynn, for uttering counterfeit Bank of England notes. "We are sorry to add that he appeared sensible for many minutes after he was turned off, and a large effusion of blood gushed from his mouth and nose, which rendered the scene most awful, terrible, and distressing.

DECEMBER.

A serious affray occurred at Horsford between two Excise officers, assisted by two privates of the 3rd Dragoon Guards, and 30 smugglers. The officers had seized a large quantity of smuggled goods at Cawston, and the smugglers succeeded in retaking only a small part. One of the soldiers was shot; several of the smugglers were desperately wounded, and two died of their wounds.

"The Lord Nelson Coach, from London to Fakenham. The coach leaves the Crown, Fakenham, on Sunday, Tuesday, Thursday, and Saturday; sups at Cambridge, and arrives in London about seven in the morning. From the Golden Cross, same days, at six in the evening."

Prices of corn at the end of the year: Wheat, 70s. to 76s. Rye, 36s. Barley, 40s. to 42s. per quarter. Oats, 20s. to 24s. Malt, 32s. per coomb. Best flour, £3 1s. 8¼d per sack. Coals, 40s. 4d. per chaldron.

1802.

JANUARY.

In 1802, the cottages were owned by William True, a whitesmith, hence the name of the Kings Lyn Museum. True's Yard, home of King's Lynn's old fishing community, the North End. Each town and village had a distinct pattern, so if a fisherman drowned at sea he could be identified. The patterns were handed down from mother to daughter.

In 1802, the cottages were owned by William True, a whitesmith, hence the name of the Museum.

There was no running water, no electricity and no drainage. The cottages were lit either by oil lamps or candles. A coal fire heated downstairs; at the end of the day the remaining hot coals were used to warm the tiny bedrooms. Chamber pots would be emptied in the nearby river.

The Duke of Bedford, Lord Paget, and Lord John Thynne, with four other gentlemen, on a visit to Lord Cholmondeley at Houghton, "had the greatest day's sport ever known in Norfolk. They killed altogether 165 hares, 42 pheasants, 5 rabbits, 2 woodcock, and 2 partridges, and this notwithstanding that the woods had been beat five times this season.

A reduction of 3s. 6d. in the pound poor-rates announced. The mulct was fixed at 7s. in the pound. "For the last 30 years there have not been so few paupers in the two workhouses, principally owing to the manufacturers of Norwich having such large orders to execute that hands are actually wanted.

The thermometer "very near to 0 (32 degrees below freezing point).".

The following Coach advertisements were published on this date:— "Royal Lynn Mail Coach sets out daily from the Duke's Head Inn, Lynn, by way of Brandon, Barton Mills, Newmarket, Bournbridge, and Epping, to the White Horse, in Fetter Lane, whence it returns every day at three o'clock." "The Fakenham and Swaffham Light Post Coach sets out daily from the Red Lion, in Fakenham, at two o'clock, and returns from London as above." "The Lord Nelson Coach, from Lynn to Norwich in seven hours. From the Globe, Lynn, to the King's Head, Norwich, every Monday, Wednesday, and Friday, returning Tuesday, Thursday, and Saturday at seven o'clock each morning." "The Lynn and Norwich Machine, from the Crown Tavern, Lynn, to the White Swan, Norwich. Runs three times a week. Insides, 12s.; outsides, 7s.

MARCH

News was received of the Definite Treaty of Peace having been signed at Amiens, on March 27th, by the Marquis Cornwallis and Buonaparte. The Norwich Loyal Military Associations assembled at St. Andrew's Hall. "Instead of field-pieces and ammunition waggons the martial divisions were preceded in their march from the Hall to the Market Place by two brewers' drays, laden with six barrels of Norwich porter, which were drunk with much joy."

APRIL.

William Dunnett, for horse stealing, and John Saunders, for stealing a cow, were executed at Thetford.

The whole of the French and Dutch prisoners confined in Yaxley Barracks were last week put on board different vessels in Lynn harbour, from whence they proceeded to their respect.

"Bear Baiting. Henry Gerrard respectfully informs the public that there will be a Bear Baiting in a meadow belonging to the Ferry Farm House, Great Yarmouth, on Monday next, the 19th inst., in the afternoon. Admission 1s.; 6d. to be returned in liquor." (The baiting was prevented by the action of the county justices.)

MAY.

A *fête* was held in Reffley Wood, near Lynn. A "fine Norfolk sheep" was roasted for the feast, presided over by Sir Martin ffolkes.

A heavy fall of snow, which in many places lay more than an inch thick upon the ground. On the 15th there was a severe frost, and snow fell for two hours. At Langley and other places it was between three and four inches in depth.

A fire occurred at Swanton paper mill, a great part of which was destroyed, with all the paper. The damage was estimated at £4,000.

JUNE.

Holkham Sheep Shearing commenced. A new thrashing machine was exhibited. An improved drill for turnip sowing was also shown. "From the same barrel seed and oilcake manure are delivered into one tube, through which it is deposited in the earth by the same coulters."

AUGUST.

August 14th 1802
We hear from Brussels that a party of gentlemen from Lynn have reached that city in the Hebe pleasure yacht. This being the first vessel that ever displayed the British flag in Brussels the quay of the port has been crowded with spectators looking at her.

August 28th William Rix was executed on Castle Hill, Norwich, for sheep stealing.

Finally:-
The Disbursements of William Mitchell and Thomas Swann Overseers of the Parish of Tuttington from Michaelmas 1802 to Easter 1803.

Payments to poor   **1802**

Oct

Paid for Benjamin Culleys Things   Allen James   Swann John   Starling William   Rounce Joseph   Widow Fish   Widow Haine   Widow Gooch   Widow Frances   Fish Catherine   Dyke Amy   Timbers Joseph   Culley Thomas   Woodrow Thomas   Howard Daniel Senr   Howard Daniel Junr   Benjamin Culley in Need   Norwich Collectioners   James Woolsey

Courtesty of https://www.gutenberg.org & https://foxearth.org.uk/ 1802NorfolkChronicle.html,

https://www.britishnewspaperarchive.co.uk/search/results? https://www.archives.norfolk.gov.uk/help-with-your-research/local-history/great-yarmouth- https://www.genuki.org.uk/big/eng/NFK/Tuttington/Poorpay_1804

THE END.

Memories
Of
Yesterday

"Duchess", built by Landamore in 1924 (length 43ft., beam 10ft.,
licensed to carry 30 passengers).

OLD SHUCK

Many a ghost story is hidden in East Anglia, this one will make even the most hardened soul quiver, the ghostly dog who has wandered the dark lanes and windswept coasts of East Anglia for centuries, so when you're coming out of the pub alone on a winters night and the wind is howling, is it the wind or old Shuck!

Shuck is a creature out of legend, but people still say that they see him today - a fiery-eyed fiend to a friendly walking companion, from a headless dog with saucer eyes (!) to a Labrador who shrank to the size of a cat. He's a cunning canine, is Black Shuck: he's not always black, and he's not always a canine! Is he your dog, your canine friend?

It seems to be well accepted that his name probably derives from the Old English Scucca or Sceocca, which means the Devil, But it could equally come from the dialect word shucky, meaning shaggy, one of Shuck's legendary physical characteristics.

In East Anglia, the earliest account we have of a supernatural dog on the loose is Abraham Fleming's 1577 tract 'A Strange and Terrible Wonder', telling of the events of Sunday August 4th in that year, when a "black dog, or the divel in such a likeness", wrought havoc and death during a dreadful storm in the parish churches of first Bungay, and then Blythburgh, both in Suffolk.

Holinshed's 'Chronicle', Stow's 'Annals' and contemporary church records all mention the awful storm and its effects, but none mention the dog. It seems reasonable to suppose that Fleming added the supernatural element, giving him the opportunity to more vividly rail against the 'sinfulness' of his times, and make a call for repentance lest God strike them with even more fearful retribution.

In the early 1950's, a young woman and her future husband were idling on the Coltishall side of the bridge at nightfall. Walking towards them from 'Coltishall Island', a triangle of land with a petrol station on it, at the meeting of three roads they saw a black dog, so large, that at first the woman thought it was a pony. As it passed them, the dog turned its head towards them, but continued, and faded away before it reached the other side. Both witnesses were very scared by the encounter but managed to cross the bridge themselves soon afterward. The woman still thinks of the incident with fear every time she must use the bridge.

Late one night between 1960 and 1962, two RAF officers were travelling by car back from Norwich to RAF Coltishall. Passing over Coltishall bridge, they turned left into the High Street and were quickly forced into a sudden stop as "an enormous black dog" crossed the road from left to right in front of them. "As it loped across our line of sight it slowly turned its head, to glare directly and disdainfully into our astonished faces, presenting us with a pair of fiery red eyes. It then slowly swung back its head and continued its measured progress onto the cobbles (if my recall of the village is sound) that stretched up to the shops/houses on the far side of the road. As it hit the cobbles it quite literally vanished." "To put it bluntly, it was a perfectly proportioned giant black dog."

The two officers looked at each other in disbelief, then sped off to the air base.

Further even as far away as west "The year was 1856 near a small village in West Norfolk, a farm labourer and his wife were walking home from a friend's house when it happened. It was a nice summers night about 10pm and just getting dark, the moon was coming up, but it was still light enough to see the countryside around them. They walked arm in arm talking as they went, when they both heard a large dog running up behind them, they stopped turned around but could not see anything, the sounds had stopped so they carried on walking. As they got closer to the front gate of their small farm cottage once again they could hear the dog but this time it was running very fast and getting so close they could hear it heavy

breathing. They now began to feel very frightened and started to run for the gate, but the dog felt as if it was on top of them, the man opened the gate first and let his wife in then slammed it shut. He turned and looked up the lane but there was nothing there and the sounds had stopped once again, he was then going to speak to his wife when a deafening howl pierced the summer night. His wife screamed and pointed to the gate, the man swung around and there it was, the biggest black dog he had ever seen, its eyes seemed to be shinning bright green. It then slowly turned and disappeared into the night; it could not be seen but it could be heard padding away into the distance."

Do you the reader live up a country lane and on your own heh heh heh.

The characteristic of invisibility inevitably leads to the question: if it was invisible, how did anyone even know that it was a dog?

The beast apparently changed its shape, which otherwise only occurs in the legends (7 instances.) A 19th century encounter led to the air being alive with 'waving flame' when a cart touched the creature, while a dog seen in about 1921 had a 'luminous glow' around it. All the details recounted up to now seem to tell us that, by and large, the more overtly paranormal aspects of Shuck have lessened over time, with the Second World War probably being a watershed, as it has proven to be in so many areas of recorded folklore.

16th century 2
17th century 3
18th century 1
19th century 23
20th century 142
21st century 10

Legends, by their very nature, are often not very precise as to where an event is supposed to happen - and surprisingly, some of the first-hand accounts aren't either listed are the results.

On road, path, track etc. 119
On marshes, marsh bank, riverbank etc. 11
In field, on common, hill etc.   9
On beach 5
In garden, grounds, park etc.   8
In church, churchyard   4
On sea cliffs 1
'Along the coast' 5
Other 2

Thus, is he often described in the literature: "He takes the form of a huge black dog, and prowls along dark lanes and lonesome field footpaths, where, although his howling makes the hearer's blood run cold, his footfalls make no sound. You may know him at once, should you see him, by his fiery eye; he has but one, and that, like the Cyclops', is in the middle of his head. But such an encounter might bring you the worst of luck: it is even said that to meet him is to be warned that your death will occur before the end of the year.

4.

And the notion that 'black dog' legends survive wherever the Vikings landed or settled simply doesn't stand up to scrutiny. There is, for instance, virtually no correlation at all between phantom dog tales and Scandinavian place names.: "Some people believe that dog-phantoms derive from [Viking] This theory is, however, untenable - at least from an historical and geographical point of view - for dog-ghosts appear prolifically in parts of England uncontaminated by Nordic beliefs."

Nowhere in Norse mythology will you find that either Odin or Thor had a dog called 'Shukr' or 'Shukir.' This is a pure invention. Indeed, (or is it)neither Odin/Woden nor Thor/ Thunor is mentioned in connection with any dog at all. Wolves yes, but not dogs. Odin had two wolves, Geri and Freki (both of which roughly mean 'greedy'), which followed him into battle.

I would like to thank Mike for allowing me this story and for emailing me
Mike Burgess.
Lowestoft, Suffolk. Website originally published January 2005. https://www.hiddenea.com/
email: mikewburgess@aol.com

THE END

MY WORLD

LOCAL ARTIST

Self Taught Artist, A man who knows colours and a man who allows JDBBooklets to use his works to portray Norfolk in its beauty . A stalham man known as "the cycling Artist'
Mr John Etheridge, well known offers the chance to buy his artwork and meet him in person, he has a facebook page too.

Life on the Land 18th &19th Norfolk

1.

By 1796, two-thirds of the county of Norfolk was used for arable farming. Whereas in the 16th and 17th centuries most of the populace owned land, many with only small holdings, a fundamental change in the agricultural situation gradually occurred during the 17th and 18th centuries. This was the change from open- field strip farming to enclosed fields (the controversial process called 'enclosure'), which had profound social as well as organisational effects.

Previously farmers often shared ploughs, horses, and manual tasks; now farms were strictly individual units with very small owners often left with unworkably smallholdings. By 1750, however, there were very few strip fields remaining, and because of private exchanges, farms were being consolidated.

The poor lost their rights to gather timber for fuel and to pasture a cow or pig on land traditionally available to them. So, the social effects were quite serious.

Enclosure of common land required legislation (and much was enclosed during the Napoleonic wars). During this period, the land-owning community consisted of 'gentlemen farmers', wealthy tenant farmers and small farmers. The first group didn't rely on farm income for their wealth and tended to have special interests like breeding pedigree livestock.

On the other hand, the rich tenant farmers worked large holdings in an intensive way and had the interest and capital to experiment with new ideas. Most farmers owned smallholdings which had often 'been in the family' for generations.

Lack of money often inhibited their interest in trying new ideas, but for them, farming was a way of life; it was 'in their blood'. Some of these latter farmers were employed by, or leased land belonging to, the wealthy estate owners.

But the proportion of landless labourers in the rural community steadily increased. Norfolk was particularly well suited to the export of grain to the continent.

By 1794, more grain was leaving the ports of Norfolk for Holland than from the whole of the rest of England. The Napoleonic wars had boosted agriculture, especially the production of grain. A huge farming effort was channelled into growing cereal crops, even in unsuitable areas, encouraged by a price escalation for grain which far outstripped that for livestock.

During the l8th and early 19th centuries, great agricultural improvements took place throughout England, with Norfolk farmers playing a significant role in both developing and publicising improved farming management and methods.

Fostered by the efforts and enthusiasm of people like Coke of Holkham and 'Turnip' Townshend, many advances were made in farming techniques, land management and machinery, and in the development of better breeds of livestock and the introduction of new and better crops. By growing turnips and artificial grasses instead of leaving land fallow, they achieved higher soil fertility. They became known across England for their progressive farming.

By 1760, turnips and clover were almost universally grown on land that previously would have been 'lain' (left) fallow, but it is uncertain just how widespread formal crop rotation was practised. Townshend and Coke evolved the famous Norfolk 'four course' system.

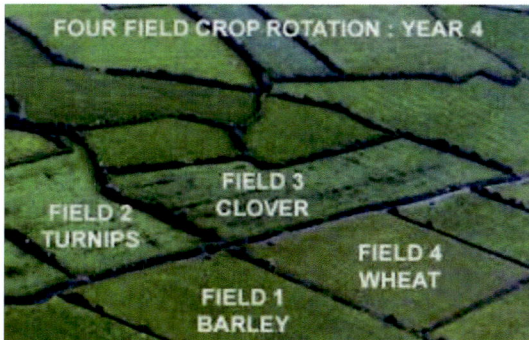

FOUR FIELD CROP ROTATION : YEAR 4

FIELD 3
CLOVER

FIELD 2
TURNIPS

FIELD 4
WHEAT

FIELD 1
BARLEY

The crops that were rotated in four groups depended somewhat on the type of soil.

For example, in the heavy land districts it was: first year fallow (either clean fallow tares, beet or turnips); second year barley; third year half clover, half peas or beans, alternately; fourth year wheat. The course on the light land districts was fallow, swedes, white turnips, mangle-wurzels, or carrots in the first year; followed by barley; then by seeds in the third year; and wheat last of all.

But there was, naturally, much variation in the order of cropping, especially among the smaller farmers.

Employment and wages in the last half of the 18th century and in the 19th century, the only major employment in Norfolk was in agriculture and the great majority of the working population was labourers on the land. Agricultural work provided many different types of employment for labourers, but they could be categorised into two main groups:

A good employer might make provision for a worker such as this, giving him or her easier or sedentary jobs, and perhaps a certain amount of charity and who stayed on the same farm or estate for long periods of time often all their working lives.

Frequently, those born on the farmland lived in a tied cottage (belonging to a particular farm).

These labourers tended to become the 'elite' of the class because they had (relative) stability of employment, and because of their permanency and great knowledge of the farm and its workings could rise from mere farmhands to become more valued farm workers, with tasks such as herdsmen or ploughmen.

Their families were born and raised there, and from an early age both sons and daughters would work on the farm, initially as bird scarers, gleaners after the harvest, cowboys and similar. As they grew up, they would enter the more 'advanced' jobs, and the women would go into the dairies, the house itself, and the tasks such as butter-making and looking after vegetable and fruit plots.

This was not always the case but was common practice. It is worth emphasising that the work wasn't contracted in the modern sense; there was absolutely no guarantee of employment. If the farm fell on hard times, or the farmer decided that he could dispense with the services of a particular labourer, then he could and would dismiss him and turn him and his family out of their cottage without compensation.

This was more likely when people grew old and infirm, and so, less useful to their employer.

Those labourers who were more mobile and contracted out their labour usually every year were the 'hired men' and 'hired women', It was the normal custom for hiring to be done once a year, at Michaelmas (29 September), the place of hiring almost always being a country fair, or, less often, a market. The fairs were frequently called 'hiring fairs' (although other business and sales would also be transacted), and they were common throughout the county.

The labourers would stand on a platform, or in an enclosure, to be 'looked over by the prospective employers for features such as strength, general appearance and character (and, in the case of girls, probably their attractiveness as well!).

They would then be questioned about their skills and abilities, their previous employment, and their liabilities (which might well include wives and children).

In the early decades of the 19th century in Norfolk, agriculture was frequently depressed and rural poverty great, so bargaining was less feasible. Skilled workers with a particularly useful trade or experience would often hire themselves on this basis because they could demand good wages, and farmers might vie with each other to get the worker they wanted.

This was the case quite often with people such as plough-team leaders and very experienced cowmen. It seems that some of the most highly valued jobs (those involved in handling livestock the team's man who looked after the horses, the yardman who cared for the cattle and the shepherd) often had a cottage made available to them.

However, during the latter part of the 18th century and into the 19th century, the trend was away from the annual 'hiring fairs', towards a more casual engagement of workers.

This was usually on a daily or weekly basis, with no pay on wet days. Later, during the Victorian era, with farm sizes increased, farmers could no longer manage with just family and some yearly engaged 'live-in' servants.

Farmers needed more labour and greater flexibility in employment, and agricultural labourers (like their industrial counterparts the factory workers) found themselves entirely at the mercy of their employers, who could reduce their pay whenever prices for their farm products dropped.

Wages for the least secure, most poorly skilled, or least experienced farm workers were very low. In a fifty-year period in the late 18th century, wages rose by only 25 per cent but the cost of living increased by 60 per cent. Labourers were in a weak bargaining position due to the over-population from which Norfolk was suffering.

Wages were usually low and were not infrequently paid in the form of goods or food, or the labourer was allowed a small plot of land to raise vegetables and perhaps to keep a pig or two. The pig was fattened and then killed in the late autumn, to be salted or smoked as a source of meat through the winter and early spring. Many a farmer gave a convincing account of such a pig-killing, and this was one of the major events in the calendar of most rural families. Everything would be used skin, bristles, bones, every scrap of meat, blood (made into puddings with oatmeal and herbs).

Wages also varied enormously between periods of plenty and periods of scarcity, and the 1820s and 1830s were, in general, a time of low wages in East Anglia. This was particularly so in this county because the woollen industry was in a state of rapid decline, as the great textile areas of northern England flourished. With alternative employment not readily available, it led to an excess of agricultural workers.

Underpinning support for the poor, was the Old Poor Law (i.e., pre-1834). The Act of Settlement of 1662 gave every individual a legal place of settlement. A parish or township was legally bound to provide him or her with poor relief in the event of their becoming destitute through old age, unemployment, or other personal circumstances.

Workhouses, the earliest of which was built in 1767, the poor had to live and work, undertaking spinning for outside (mostly Norwich) manufacturers.

In some, just the women and children worked indoors while the men were engaged on nearby farms. By 1834, half of the parishes of Norfolk had access to a 'poor-house' as they were sometimes called. After this date it was common for families and married couples to be separated. The conditions of the agricultural labourer reached a very low ebb by 1815, but things got worse.

The end of the wars meant that many ex-soldiers were unemployed, grain prices fell, and farmers lowered wages; a landowner- dominated Parliament passed the Corn Laws, which prevented the import of grain, until the price of English wheat reached 80 shillings a quarter.

It is not surprising, therefore that discontent, fuelled by steep rises in the prices of bread and flour during the post-Napoleonic wars depression, led to violence.

Rioting occurred in 1816, with the anger directed at property, machinery. Ricks (stacks of hay, corn, or peas, often thatched [roofed with straw] for weather protection) were burned and threshing machines broken. The latter were depriving labourers of valuable winter employment and consequently were much hated.

Further rioting broke out in 1830 as again farm workers demanded rises in wages and the abolition of threshing machines, twenty-nine of which were smashed.

As the population continued to rise, under employment became worse and consequently, poor rates had to be increased, leading to strong moves among ratepayers for all relief to the poor outside of workhouses to be abolished.

This national reform movement resulted in the 1834 Poor Law Amendment Act, which led to eighteen new Poor Law Unions and twelve new workhouses being established in Norfolk.

The paupers found themselves being divided into groups based on age, sex and state of health, and were supervised in their extremely tedious and repetitive work and in their living areas by a very watchful 'master. The 1834 Act took little account of the needs of the sick, especially of the mentally sick, and many 'harmless idiots' were living amongst the general pauper population in the union houses.

The appointment of Poor Law medical officers considerably improved the standards of care for the sick poor, certainly above that of the village quacks to whom they would have previously turned for cheap treatment.

The Poor Law Guardians had very hard and at times inhumane attitudes to the poor, probably regarding their condition as being their own fault, and their continued existence as a costly nuisance to those who had to contribute to their support.

On estates where the demand for labour exceeded the cottage accommodation, gangs of workers were brought in from elsewhere. They came from other villages, which were not controlled by the one landlord where speculators erected rows of poor cottages and charged exorbitant rents because of the shortage of housing.

Labourers from these villages would often travel quite a distance to where the work was offering and be formed into work gangs by 'gang masters'. These organisers could offer such gangs for hire to farmers to do various types of work such as weeding, potato digging and turnip hoeing.

The work they had using the traditional methods was arduous, long, repetitive, and not always regular. For example, before the drill method of sowing turnips became the norm, they were sown broadcast or fleet on the ground. When this was secured by a leather band which went round his neck. He took the small seed between his finger and thumb and sowed in step; that is, as his left foot came up, his left hand dipped into the seed bowl and scattered the seed.

Turnip seed was sown at the rate of half a pint an acre and if the sower dug too deeply into his bowl with his thumb and forefinger he would not make his seed last.

Not more than one or two men on each farm could sow at the necessary rate with two hands. Most men were only able to sow with one. This was necessarily slower, but the sower who used one hand only was able to carry a seed-hod - a bigger container - on one side of his body.

Clover and mustard were sown in the same way as turnips. When the turnips came up, it would be some time during the harvest; and the men would be set to hoe in the early morning before breakfast when the dag or dew would still be on the corn.

They would likewise hoe turnips when a damp or wet day compelled them to make a break in the harvesting.

It was a hard job hoeing plants that grew from broadcast seed, and they would have to hoe twice; the second time to cut out the knots or concentration of plants and the weeds that had grown since the first hoeing.

Traditionally, the method of harvesting the grain crop was by hand, using a sickle. Thirty-four men mow the wheat and to lay it evenly their scythes are fitted with cradles made of iron rods. These men are each followed by two women ...... and a boy or girl to gather up the corn into small sheaves.

Eight teams' men .... follow to shock up the sheaves of which they place ten in a shock ...... 300 acres of wheat is cut in six days. Carting takes a further eight. Eighteen to 20 days are needed to complete the harvest.

The women mentioned previously, were usually the wives of the harvest workers and were called gavellers. Their job was to rake the mown corn into gavels or rows ready for tying into sheaves, or for carting if left loose.

Barley was often left 'on the gavel'. The stubbles are dew- raked by men drawing a long iron-toothed rake. A tool called a shack-fork a fork with curved tines and an iron bow at the shoulder was used to gather the swathes of barley into gavels ready for pitching onto the wagons.

A gaveller worked behind each wagon feeding the corn to two men one on each side of the wagon who did the pitching while another two men on top of the load received the corn and arranged it evenly.

The man paid the gaveller about a shilling a day: if she had a young child to look after at the same time, she would have to manage as best she could. Men, women, lads, boys, and girls all worked in the fields, and each had certain jobs and set wages.

What was the difference between a boy and a lad'? The lad got more money than the boys: he was, in fact, older and would not he call a lad until he had left school. While he was still at school, he was a boy until he was seventeen or eighteen, he would be called a lad. A lad who had not long left school would be taken on at harvest time as a half-man. That is, he received half a man's wages. He did very light jobs during the harvest: taking the loaded wagons to the stack yard; or drag-work, leading a horse with the drag-rake.

The horses he handled would he the staid old jobbing horses that had lost all their sprightliness after long years of hard ploughing. When a lad was sixteen or seventeen, he was taken on as a three-quarter man, getting three-quarters of a man's wages. He did all the jobs a full man did except pitching, the handling of the sheaves of corn from the ground on to the wagon the heaviest job of all.

A three-quarter man was usually stationed on top of the load. After the corn was cut and carted it was stored in huge wooden eighteenth-century barns for storing and processing.

Norfolk farmers liked to keep most of their crop indoors rather than stacking it in a yard.

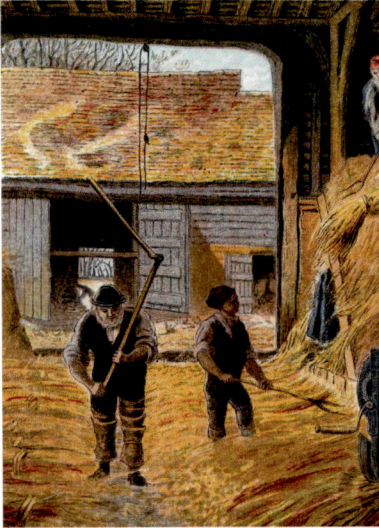

Despite constant improvements to the design of threshing machines and its increasingly widespread use on many farms in the 1840s, the crop was still being hand-flailed, a handy activity for otherwise idle hands in the winter.

The threshing was done on the middle- stead, the middle of the barn, the floor of which was paved with clay-daub (dab) which was clay beaten down until it became as hard as concrete. The threshing was done with a flail, or frail, which had an ash handle with a swivel on top. The part that struck the corn was called the swingle and was made of tough wood, like holly or blackthorn. It was attached to the swivel on the handle by thongs of snakeskin, or eel-skin using a knot of special design.

When using the flail, the thresher swung the handle over his shoulder and brought down the swingle across the straw just below the ears so that the grains of corn were shaken out without being bruised. Great skill was needed to use the flail consistently effectively - it was very easy for an inexperienced thresher to hit himself on the back of the neck.

While the threshing was being done the big double doors at one end of the barn and the single door at the other end were opened to allow the through draught to blow away the dust. After the threshing was completed the Sievers job was to separate the caving's from the grain and chaff, the grain being piled at one side of the middle stead.

A scuppit (a wooden casting shovel) was then used to throw the grain high in the air, the heavy grains falling furthest away and the lighter ones dropping short forming a kind of tail. Thus, these inferior grains became known as tailings; they have mostly ever been used for cattle feed.

One of the skills that had the highest acclaim in the East Anglian countryside under the old farm economy was the ability to draw or plough a straight furrow and lay a level stetch (a section of ploughed land) so that it looked like a well-made length of corduroy. So great was the interest in ploughing a well-finished stetch with mathematically straight furrows, and so keen was the rivalry between various horsemen that, even after they had spent most of an autumn day ploughing an acre or so in the field, they would spend the rest of it ploughing the land over once again in the cosiness of the inn bar.

But the farmworker was practised in numerous skills as well as ploughing and drilling. These other skills included stacking, thatching, hedging, ditching, and looking after the horses.

Accommodation for agricultural workers was generally unsatisfactory, with crowded and sub-standard conditions being the norm. It was mostly supplied by employers and almost never owned by the labourers themselves.

The settlement laws which made the local populace of each village responsible for those born, or claiming a settlement in that parish, contributed to the lack of new dwellings erected and the decay of older ones. Typical dwellings in the early nineteenth century were quite dilapidated being held up with wooden shoring and having decayed sagging roofs.

It was not uncommon for one-bedroom houses to have seven to ten inhabitants. In northern Norfolk, especially, Morston and Saxlingham are good examples flintstone was the predominant building material, so the few better homes were made of flint and brick with a pantile roof. Around Binham, many buildings were built of limestone, as large quantities were available from the ruins of the Priory, which became the village quarry.

By the 1840s most people lived in a one or two-roomed cottage with, perhaps, a scullery or back-house added on. Most also had a shed for livestock attached to the house, all being set in a small plot of land used for vegetables and as a hen and pig run. There would have been no sanitation of any sort, unless the cottage happened to be near a stream or pond, which case would have been used. Otherwise, a hole in the garden or a pail or tub in the house, emptied often, and used to manure the garden.

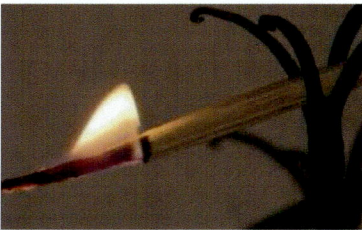

More prosperous families had candles, and oil lamps perhaps, but most workers homes were lit by rush lights- rushes stripped to expose the pithy centre and then dipped in melted tallow (greasy remnants of animal fat) which burned dimly and smoky and gave out a vile smell. And, of course, such light as was given out by a fire of wood (no coal, except in port towns and perhaps in some of the small coastal villages with harbours).

The fire also provided the only means of cooking, with ranges and other 'cooking stoves' not appearing until late in the 19th century. Due to these conditions Pollution and contamination were widespread, and produced terrible recurring epidemics of diarrhoea, gastric disorders, and fevers, with typhoid a frequent visitor, and, after its first appearance in 1832.

Milk was scarce, with most being made into butter or cheese, in any case, as it would not keep, so water and ale were the most common drinks, ale, being processed, was much safer than polluted water. They ate large amounts of coarse bread, perhaps with cheese or pork dripping, or the crackling from pork skin occasionally.

Vegetables were eaten often but there was not much variety - cabbage and carrots mostly; with potatoes becoming more general in the early 19th century.

In addition, onions, and garlic (despite alleged English hostility to them!), boiled wheat and a great deal of pot barley used in stews and soups. Fish was a more regular item in the diets of coastal people, but some was transported inland to supplement that caught in the larger rivers.

Rabbits and game birds were eaten with great relish whenever available.

The great estates like Holkham were jealously guarded, as many a time the rich had fragrant stews and had to be hidden in the roof or at the bottom of the garden while the gamekeeper was in the neighbourhood.

In some areas of Norfolk great rabbit warrens were maintained, and these afforded the determined poacher good potential.

But the penalties were extremely severe, and execution or transportation was very common. It was often said that one was more likely to be hanged for killing a rabbit than for killing a fellow human being! So, diet was plain, monotonous, and cheap, and reasonably healthy provided there was enough of it.

Villages by the hundred still exist in Norfolk many not all that changed in appearance from how they looked one hundred and fifty years ago, and longer. Take away the bitumen roads, vehicular road signs, phone boxes, telephone and power lines, television aerials, the few modern homes and buildings and the odd modern advertising signs, and one could visualise closely their traditional state.

'village life' meant a unique kind of isolation from the rest of the world, for the village and its surrounding farms were a 'villagers' world.

As it is in the authors village of Walsingham.

It meant knowing and being known by everyone else in the village. It meant knowing quite clearly one's station in life and what this entitled one to do or to be, even how and with whom one could and should go about. It meant finding one's entertainment, such as it was, in the village or within walking distance of it. Church activities and involvement meant a great deal to a considerable proportion of the village inhabitants, and the annual Sunday School outing was for many children the only or most eagerly awaited treat of the year.

For those women not forced through necessity to work some or all the time in the fields, village life meant being tied to the home all day every day, their monotony relieved by a regular succession of 'packmen', 'tally men', itinerant traders calling at the kitchen door with groceries, hats, crockery, brushes, underwear, ribbons, etc. Nobody bought or sold fruit, flowers, vegetables, plants - one exchanged, bartered, begged, or gave them away.

The same with pig 'fry'. Speaking the local dialect,(He say thus merkanical Hoss or suffin) and distrusting or despising anyone who did not - except the parson and the schoolmaster.

It meant going to the toilet in a dark and draughty privy at the bottom of the garden or at the back of the house. It meant going to bed early to economise in lamp-oil and coal; washing in cold water from pump or well; eating cold fat bacon for breakfast or going without. It meant finding your way across fields and along deserted lanes in the dark, and enjoying it, especially if you were courting. All that, and very much more, are what 'village life' used to mean.

So next time you drive past a farm with seagulls following a tractor cast your mind back to the 18th&19th century, life was hard, very hard, and women worked the fields then, and had to cook, clean, and sow and knit.

Norfolk may be a fare land, but folk have worked hard to bring East Anglia into being.

THE END

Growing Up In Caston

1.

This story is Part Two of Linda's life from playing in the fields around her home to now, but we must relate briefly to the first chapter a surprise to Linda and her memories.

Caston is a small peaceful village with a green and an attractive partly thatched church.

It lies deep in the heart of rural West Norfolk just three miles from the picturesque village of Thompson which has many thatched houses.

In 1953 Mr John "Jack" Creed, his wife and children Peggy, Jacqueline and Linda moved to the end cottage nearest the road.

In 1955 the two cottages were joined to become one.

Jacqueline says that at lambing time her father slept in his isolated shepherd's hut at night if he had too. This hut was a wooden hut on wheels that stood close to the track leading westwards from the road at the top of the hill.

When I was 4 maybe nearly 5 my sister Josephine was born, we nicknamed her (Joey). Mum looked after her, while we my older sister Jacqueline and I used to take sandwiches, cutting a direct route across the meadows.

Lambing might keep him up all night and Jacqueline remembers her father walking home before dawn with a Tilly lamp, carrying baby lambs under his arm if they were too big to fit in his pockets

The lambs, which looked half dead, would be put in the garden shed under an infra-red lamp and would be bottle-fed that was nice to watch them drink their mother's milk until they were strong enough to return to the meadows.

Peter Childerhouse tells how he (Mr Creed) would walk in front of the flock and how, as in Biblical times, the sheep would follow him. On one occasion, as a teenager, Peter and his sheepdog took about 250 hoggets' (yearling sheep) there on their own, the destination was Black Rabbit Warren, which is in Wrentham parish. the dog being aware if a sheep tried to abscond from the flock.

I have used Linda's words where possible, she says " From a young age she will always remember being with her beloved father and helping where possible, with his beloved sheep, and helping her mother who worked hard.

The children were surrounded by fields and streams. This is what this story is about, love, and devotion to a man that would become well known in the village, her mother's love and her life and friendships formed too, happiness and sadness in her days that she remembers fondly.

Her father 'Jack' worked for a Mr Beales and was his Shepard, Mr Beales the farmer allowed her and her friends to venture forth and have walks, paddling in the stream, picking primroses and to roam as free as we liked.

Her sisters Peggy, Jackie, and she always loved picking primroses for their mum who they loved and cherished , and Mother's day was no exception.

Every other Sunday they had to attend Sunday School at the church in Caston.

After singing and on their way home, the aroma of mum's cooking used to waft into their young nostrils, the aroma from the kitchen was a dream of lure, mum she said was a good cook and would cook Bread cakes, Sausage rolls and a beautiful Roast Dinner with all the trimmings. If we were having pork, she would soak it in water overnight to get rid of any salt. Hams too, mother was a genius.

Before mum married she was a cook in a Bakers, so we always had lovely meals . Sundays we always had trifles for pudding.

Teatime was not only for food but a bath , no fancy bath for us, we had a tin bath in front of a coal fire, which we giggled and splashed in the water that her mother kept topping up, and for heating our beds a lovely copper tray was put in our beds to get the sheets warm, so that bedtimes we could snuggle up and dream out adventures next day. My other sisters used to bathe in the bath near the fire. If father wasn't with his sheep he too would watch over his girls carefully.

At this tender age I had to start school and walk O.6 miles to Caston Primary just over half a mile with my two older sisters Jackie and Peggy. all weathers, wind, rain, hail, sleet, and snow.

With intrigue like youngsters have I started making friends with some of the other children of the village. A friendship formed and would blossom with Ann and Kate

who lived up the hill, close to us in one of Mr Beales Houses.

Life was full of adventures, and we didn't realise that time was ticking, we all became great friends, the adventures in our young lives took us all over Caston and into exploration, we were more like tomboys than young ladies.

Primary school days were so much fun as well and we went on nature walks, and we found all many of creepy crawlies, but then wintertime came, the little creatures were back in their homes as we were, snug and warm. Although we were taught all about nature and why it was part of living, we were growing up, and enjoying everything around us.

Winter though was cold, and we still had to walk , and by the time we got to school our feet were soaked.

We had a huge open fire, and the teacher took our socks off dried our feet and put our socks near the fire and upturned our little shoes to dry the inside as well. Winter came and went and so did spring, life was returning, leaves on the trees forming, and corn in the fields growing and soon before one knew it, it was harvest time, and more joys to behold.

Now harvest time and living in the country is hard work for the grown-ups but for us youngsters after chores were finished , we would run to the field make sure the combine harvested had finished and we would make great ole tunnels in the straw bales. We were young, we were adventurous, so we made tunnel mazes to find our way out. We could also carry them as they were light.

Mrs Lake Ann's and Kate's mother was a wonderful lady, and always welcomed me into their home, it was warm and cosy and that was cherished. From their home we would walk to Rockland to get shopping and Mrs Lake bless her always gave us money for a sweet or chocolate.

Caroline another friend I met at Caston School sometimes used to come with us on our adventures, if the locals gave us funny looks it was cos we all sounded like cackling hens.

One such Saturday night we attempted to make a tent with polythene on Mr Beales land , a night of nights, and looking back hilarious, it poured with rain, and we heard a rustling noise, shh! One said, 'there's a stream that runs close by its that! but we were not having it, we were scared, wet with the leaks coming through the holes made by the poles, yep we weren't campers, we were shivering little girls and the rustling noise was one of my father's sheep, we didn't stand and say hello we left the field quicker than we went in, and by the time we got home our beds were calling us, but mother was waiting for an explanation and a towel.

The bed was warmed by a stone hot water bottle , dad laughed, he was a shrewd man a

proper Norfolk bewty. His pronunciation, with local tongue, brought his love of animals and a living, he was a man of honesty, uprightness, courage, and patience. I loved him as did the others, I often wonder did they love him like I did!

At the age of 9 my brother John was born, now the family was 4 girls and one boy.

Mr Beale the farmer decided it was time we got rid of the tin bath and had a proper bath, the fun we had in this was a treasure of dreams. We took it down to the field and my old bewty became a boat. We sailed this bath a broom handle for a mast and an old sheet for the sail, we were the three adventurers Kate Ann and Caroline. But the old bath got holes in it, and it started to leak, it had to go father said, so then it went on the old rag and bones man's cart and into history.

 My friend Anne had a sister Kate who sadly developed MS and the symptoms are variable and unpredictable, and no two people have the same symptoms. The symptoms can fluctuate over time, one can suffer Fatigue, Walking difficulties, numbness or tingling, Vision Problems and vertigo and Dizziness. This is followed by Bladder Problems and for a female , well even a male, sexual problems such as responses are affected by damage in the central nervous system. All these degenerative health issues must have become too much for this young lady, the stresses of living with MS as well as the result of neurologic and immune changes. Anxiety, mood swings, irritability and episodes of crying posed significant challenges for Kate that at the age of only 35 she couldn't take any more and took her own life. I miss her like I do my father.

 Sadly, that time flashed by, and my other friends Anne and Kate and family moved away but we kept in touch, I cried when they went, I had so many memories.

After primary school was senior school, normal lessons to leaving age then my first job at the age of just 15 was with my friend Caroline Freston. Together we worked at Briton Brushes. The Wymondham works was one of the most up-to-date brush factories in the country with its own railway sidings, sawmills, and engineering workshops.

 In 1920 D. Matthew and Son amalgamated with S. D. Page and Sons, to form the Briton Brush Co, at Page's factory in Lady's Lane, Wymondham. There was a company at Diss too.

Much of the special machinery for brush-making was designed and made in the engineering workshops on site.

The factory took in English trees and other raw materials and produced complete and finished brush ware. I loved working there, everyone was so friendly, and I learned a lot.

 The company provided many amenities for the welfare and comfort of the men and women who worked in the factory, including a canteen, playing fields and a housing estate.

Even works outings by special excursion trains were arranged. It was the best job I ever had, I learned how to make every brush you imagined, and it was a job I looked forward to going too, however soon other sadness was to be part of my village life.

1985 The company closed. After closing the factory was pulled down to make way for housing and the estate on the former brush works site has such road names as Briton Way and Page's Way.

After working they're for a year I had to leave ,for my parents were to leave Caston after 16 years, it was a sad day. But my friend Anita's family at weekends invited me to stay there and I used to stay at Anita's in Caston with her Mum Jean, and her father Leslie and brother Nigel. So, I didn't leave all, and never see them again, I was only 10 mins away and loved going back to see them all at weekends.

The Red Lion, circa 1900

We used to frequent our local pub which I'm sure the author would like to visit if he comes from his village is the Red Lion. We all enjoyed this very quiet pub, quaint would be the operable word but fresh looking, Really nice atmosphere, excellent food at very reasonable prices. A great meld of rustic and modern, well-appointed with a great charm.

My new job j when I left Caston at the age of 16 was with Travenol Manufacture of basic pharmaceutical products.

In 1931 two Iowa doctors launched the Don Baxter Intravenous Products Company to distribute intravenous solutions commercially to hospitals in the midwestern United States.

Dr. Ralph Falk and Dr. Donald Baxter knew that the intravenous solutions available at the time were of variable quality and limited in quantity.

Baxter formed a pharmaceutical specialties division under the name Travenol Laboratories in 1949. The division was responsible for developing and marketing chemical compounds and medical equipment.

In 1976 Baxter shareholders voted to adopt the name Baxter Travenol for the parent company, with Travenol Laboratories as the major domestic operating subsidiary.

So, my job was now pharmaceutical from Brushes, but despite my lavish career my friendship was still with the girls, and we used to catch the bus and go into Norwich Saturday nights to a local dance or into the village social club at Wretham. Nigel used to go to Speedway in Kings Lyn .

More sadness was to follow in latter lives, Anita's brother Nigel a lovely person, devolved a terminal illness and at 53 he too passed away.

As the years went by we all went our separate ways, but I never forgot Jean's for having me stay at theirs and treating me like one of their own .

Sadly, for me in 2007 at the age of just 58 I lost my wonderful sister Peggy to a terminal illness which for me then and still is devastating.

I would like to say thank you to Caroline, Anne, Anita, and Janet for giving me their permission to add to my story which David has lovingly put together .

And Ladies I understand you are still in contact. Bless you all, thankyou for letting me write this.

Linda is a lovely lass her father brought her up in a family that she loved. It's been another pleasure writing this squit (not really), but she says that word reminds her of her father's dialogue so Linda by ole bewty your story has been lovingly written. Cor, blarst me! Zackly.

Keep a troshin gal Linda

Boy David.

The End

Caston Primary photo & The Red Bull Courtesy of Caston On-line and Mr V H Shubrook all other photos Linda.

Photos of harvest & Briton Brushes Http:// google.com.

EVACUEE ALFIE & Other Evacuees CAME HOME.

These are true stories and are courtesy of https://wroxhamhistory.wordpress.com/evacuee-alfie-comes-home-again/

Alfie Sparrowhawk and his brothers lived with a couple called Dick (Richard) and Ethel Mills at 4 St Marys Close Wroxham during the war.

In November 2013 a sprightly-looking Alfie, accompanied by wife Joyce, their daughter Karen, and her husband David, came back again to the village where he spent all the war years. Ethel Mills and her husband have long since passed away but what an amazing woman she was. When the dozen or so evacuees from Bethnal Green, London, got off the train at Wroxham Station in September 1939 they had to walk around a mile to the Village Hall where a group of adults waited to size them up.

Alfie was there with brothers Joe and Ernie (Henry having been evacuated to a different part of the country).

Ethel Mills, already a mother of three, picked two of the boys and said: "I'll take these two."

But quick as a flash one of them piped up: "My mum said we wasn't to be split up!"

Without any hesitation she said: "OK, then, I'll take the three."

The first thing she did when she got them home was to pull out a tin bath and put them in it one by one,

Alfie told me. For him and his brothers (Henry, who was unsettled at his first placement, joined them later) what followed were five very happy years within a truly loving family.

In fact, they only returned to their own home two years after the end of the war when the government insisted they leave and amid tears all round their much-loved substitute mother reluctantly took them to Norwich and put them on the train to London.

They'd been here so long that back home in Bethnal Green the boys used to make fun of their Norfolk accents.

As Alfie and I were at Wroxham School and in the church choir together we were able to exchange memories, particularly of poor Mr Woodward whose almost impossible task it was to get us all off the Caen Meadow each evening; and the smell of burning and the hissing sound as the village blacksmith nailed a red-hot horseshoe onto a waiting hoof.

Bobby Woodcock's name came up as also did the ever-kindly Mrs Clifford Gilbert, a fellow evacuee Irene (or Rosie) Redman, and Mr Hall, owner of one of the village shops, who according to Alfie could crack his knuckles rhythmically.

He was also able to identify his brother Henry (who unfortunately died many years ago) in the sea scout photograph, below. I hope Alfie will now be over the moon again when he sees his own name also recorded here for posterity.
Wroxham Sea Scouts kneeling from left: Keith Turner, Bob Blake, (Who's this?), Cyril

Durrant. Back row (Who's this?), Ernie Sparrowhawk, Raymond Jeckells holding the standard, (Who's this?), Kenneth Herbert who kindly provided the picture, Henry Sparrowhawk. On the right, in his ATC officer's uniform, is Mr Sutton, a scout commissioner, in whose garden, Southerhay (Now Tudor Lodge) the photograph was taken. On the left are two of his four children: Caroline, known as Lindy, and Richard.

SAD NEWS *came to original writer of this story, for in the summer of 2015: Alfie had passed away.*

MORE EVACUEE MEMORIES

In November 2016 Marilyn Hughes emailed Wroxham history to say:- My father, John Lucas, was evacuated to Wroxham during the war from Bethnal Green. He lived with Mr and Mrs Durrant and their son Basil and has many fond memories of his time spent in Norfolk.

The Durrants lived in a tied cottage at Hoveton Hall where Mr Durrant was a woodman for the estate. The Durrants' son Basil worked in a boatyard in Wroxham and dad kept in touch with the family for years. When Mrs Durrant died, dad went to her funeral and was mentioned in the local paper as an evacuee paying his respects.

Originally his class from Colombia Road School, Bethnal Green, were evacuated to North Walsham. A fortnight later some grammar schoolboys were also evacuated there. As the town had a grammar school, it was thought they should be given preference over the Bethnal Green evacuees, so dad and half of his class were sent to Hoveton Hall.

Captain Clark was the owner of the hall, and his secretary was a Mr Barnes, who set up a school for them in a garage. Their teacher was Mr Hawkes and Captain Clark bought him a bicycle so he could get to the hall from his lodgings.

Dad says he went to the Durrants with Bobby Lane, but Bobby went home before long.

The rest of the boys were Ingram, Merryman, Browning, Bowie, Shakespeare, Eric Parkes and Badman (he cannot remember most of the Christian names!) Mr Barnes's son was also taught with them.

Dad thinks he was there from Sept 1939 until June 1940. He was then sent to Cheshire, as it was thought they were too near the coast in Norfolk.

Another email to https://wroxhamhistory.wordpress.com from Jean Jones (formerly Jean

Ingram) from Albuquerque, New Mexico, on January 10, 2017:-

My brother Ron* was among the boys evacuated to Hoveton Hall very early in the war but my Mum thought I'd be a hindrance so kept me at home!

After the Hoveton evacuees were moved to Cheshire, Ron wrote home to say what a horrible place it was where he and a friend were staying. When they ran away and hitchhiked back to London their clothes were so dirty their mothers burned them! That's when Mr Clark wrote and told Mum to choose six boys to go back to the hall as his "guests for the duration of the war."

Mum and I visited Ron and she became friends with Mrs. Rushmore, where my cousins John and Stan were billeted, and Mrs. Hayward, who took in another cousin Beatrice, known as Bunny.

When the Station Road cottage in Hoveton became empty Dad got the use of a small van and, having applied and been accepted by the Kings Head folk who owned the property, we packed what we could get into the van and moved to Norfolk.

We left a lot of furniture, etc., behind for scavengers in London – many men grew wealthy that way! The only thing I missed was the piano. I don't remember ever denying being an evacuee [as a mutual friend Bram Lowe had claimed] but did consider myself a misplaced person. The same when I came here as a GI bride.

I remember visiting the hall in those days, especially running up and down the stairs with Patsy Barnes, who was my age. Her brother Dougal and Ron kept in touch until, along with Mr Clark, they emigrated to Africa in 1947.

Ron stayed at the hall until Mum, and I settled in Station Road and Ron went on to the Paston Grammar School. Dad was billeted on the west coast manufacturing arms. Mrs Rushmore – a lovely lady, with no children of her own – kept in touch with my cousins up until her death. She was always called Auntie Rushie, even by me and Ron.

*Sadly, J*ean's brother Ronald Ingram passed away just after Christmas 2016.*

EVACUEE IVY'S VERY MIXED MEMORIES

I very often get enquiries relating to Wroxham which turn out to be about Hoveton. Such was the case when Steve Dowsett got in touch about his mother, whom he was bringing from her home in Hornchurch to Norfolk on a nostalgic visit. So, if the station in Hoveton was called Wroxham, and the largest village store in the world is called Roy's of Wroxham, why should I quibble? I was very happy to meet up with Steve, his wife Jackie and his lively 88-year-old mum, Ivy. And what a tale she had to tell!

Bethnal Green's Columbia School pupils outside Pioneer House. Ivy is the smiling blonde girl in the centre of the back row; Joyce is second from the right.

When nine-year-old evacuee Ivy Grover left her Bethnal Green, London, home in September 1939 she said she didn't feel too sad because she was told she was only going for a night. Which is why when she arrived at Hoveton Assembly Rooms, with her fellow pupils and teachers from Columbia Road School, she had only a nightdress and toothbrush in a brown paper parcel.

At the Assembly Rooms [later Rivett's Garage, later still demolished to make way for an

expanded Roy's Grocery Store] the children were given food parcels and, to their joy, a large bar of chocolate each before the ladies of the village decided who they would "billet". Mrs Gertrude Wade of Meadow Drive had stated that she wanted a fair-haired girl and a dark-haired girl, so it was lucky that blonde Ivy, who was chosen first, had been teamed for the journey with brunette Joyce Farmer, aged just eight.

Mrs Wade

At their new Hoveton home the girls met Mr Wade, whose name Ivy remembered as Bertie, and their two daughters, Marion, and Joan (later to marry JRE Draper, the local estate agent and auctioneer 1934-1944). They would remain living in great comfort with this family for 11 months.

The first thing Mrs Wade did was to take them shopping for completely new outfits. She also told them that although they would be going to school with their fellow pupils at Pioneer House [the former name of the first property after Roy's carpark directly opposite Hoveton Police Station] she did not want the girls mixing with them at any other time.

"She was posh, you see," says Ivy.

Meanwhile Ivy's mother, who had to work six days a week to feed and clothe her young family after her husband had died when Ivy was three, was suffering the extra strain of living in wartime London.

It was then that Mrs Wade decided the poor woman needed a break and started knocking on doors in the village until she found someone willing to take her in for a few days.

The volunteers were the Heywood family and Ivy stayed there with her mother for a blissful week's holiday.

In August 1940 it was decided that Hoveton was too dangerously close to Yarmouth and the evacuees were transferred somewhere safer.

Before Ivy and Joyce left for Staffordshire, Mrs Wade, who had banked the 10s 6d* a week she had been paid for each of the girls, gave it to them as a parting gift.

In Staffordshire Ivy and Joyce were chosen by a brother and sister to billet on their farm, which was a long walk across fields to their school. The brother wore milk bottle glasses, which to the young girls gave him a sinister appearance. It was the start of a most unhappy time.

Their bedroom ran across the top of the farm with sacks of corn stacked along one wall.

These attracted the mice, which came out at night, even scampering over their bed.

"We had to sleep with our heads under the covers", says Ivy. Every day they were fed on rabbit followed by rhubarb, unless the farmers had guests, in which case there was suddenly a good array of food.

Even worse for the pre-teen girls, there was no bathroom, so they were bathed in a dolly tub in front of the fire with the brother sitting in a nearby armchair. When they objected, the sister said: "He's not looking at you – he's reading his newspaper". But he was looking, Ivy told me.

The girls complained about all these incidents to their headmistress, but she believed they were making it up.

"You can't expect the best billet all the time just because you had that in Hoveton," was always her answer.

Things came to a head over Ivy's feet. Taken on a visit to a neighbouring farm, the mud was so thick that Ivy's shoes were dragged off and couldn't be rescued so the farmer's wife found her an old pair of boots to wear.

The zips were so rusty that she couldn't undo them at bedtime and the brother told her to sleep in them because he could not cut them off as they were someone else's property.

At school the following morning the headmistress called her into her study to ask why she was wearing boots. When she explained, she took a pair of scissors and cut them off Ivy's swollen feet. It was then that she realised the girls had been telling the truth all along, visited the farm and ended their stay there.

She was very apologetic about not believing them earlier but said she didn't have anywhere else to place them.

Joyce's brother, who was in the Army, arrived to take her home. Fortunately for Ivy, on their walk to school they had often met a friendly couple who used to tell them that if the girls ever needed anywhere to stay, they would love to have them. And that's where she spent the rest of her stay in Staffordshire.

At the end of 1941, Ivy returned home but she was so terrified by the bombing that earlier the next year she asked to be evacuated again. Joyce decided to join her, and they were sent to Leicestershire… but that's another story.

*10s6d a week is 52.5p in decimal currency, with spending power of about £16 today

FOOTNOTE:- Many children from towns and cities had never been to the countryside. Unlike today, children did not have television programmes to show them what to expect. In fact, one child who left London for Norfolk in 1939 asked: 'Are we still in England?'.

REMEMBERING IVY

On January 22, 2018, Ivy's son Steve phoned with the sad news that his mother had passed away at the age of 89. He went on to say that she had been so delighted with the account on this website(https://wroxhamhistory.wordpress.com) her adventures as an evacuee that he'd had it framed for her wall. Now this memento will be passed down to future generations of her family – and they'll learn what an intrepid little survivor she had been.

LINDA'S SEARCH FOR DOWN THE HILL

On February 19, 2020, Linda Vincent wrote I have for some time been trying to find the exact location of Down The Hill and thanks to your wonderful website(https://wroxhamhistory.wordpress.com). I now have the answer. My grandmother was Mrs Louisa Ellis and she lived at 19 Malthouse Hill with my mother, Doris, her sister Lou (Louisa) and her son Eddie Manning.

My mother was evacuated from Bethnal Green in WW2 and stayed with a few families before her mother moved to Wroxham and they moved Down The Hill.

My mother's memories are a bit sketchy but one of the people she stayed with as an evacuee was Colonel Charles who is mentioned in one of your posts. I have driven down the avenue with my mother several times, but she has not been able to identify the house she stayed in.

(Editor's note: Wroxham House was demolished in the Sixties for the Charles Close estate. It stood on the site of numbers 76 and 78.)

My mother can remember that that his maid used to take her to the cinema. She can also remember attending school at the Church Hall with the other village children. To start with there were too many children because of the number of evacuees and she only attended part time. This changed once several evacuees returned home.

My mother is still referred to as The Evacuee today! Sadly, I cannot remember my grandmother as I was only three when she passed away, but from all accounts she was quite a character. My mother learned to

8.

swim in the river at the Caen Meadow and recalls how the swans used to knock on the back window of their cottage, which was right on the river front, to be fed each day.

After they were fed they hissed at her.

At some point after this my grandmother moved to Nobel Crescent as I believe some of the other residents did.

THE END

wwmm.org for tin bath
en.wilkapedia.org Hoverton Hall
Map data Google.com
Paston college North Walsham Archive

If you have any stories of your childhood life, and village life and wish to have it printed to become recorded for posterity, please contact the author david464u@icloud.com JDBBooklets. Thank You.

Anyone remember these lads &. Lasses

THE END

Saturday at Wroxham

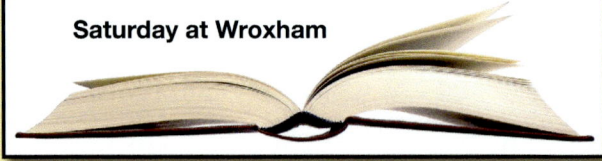

So many boats upon the river!
So many pennants all a-quiver!
So many yachts about the quays,
So many sails amongst the trees;
So many people everywhere,
So much holiday in the air!
The half-past one from Liverpool Street
So filled up to the very last seat,
And people pour our of the station
Filled with holiday jubilation:
Hurrah! Hurrah! We're here! We're here!
Luggage, luggage, everywhere -
So many come with one accord,
So many innocents abroad!
Take my luggage down to Presses' -
Do you know what Bunn's address is?
-
What time do the buses go -
How can I find Brimbelow?
Hurry! Hurry! Lose no tricet
Time is flying, we may miss it!
Thus they treat with Time the fawner,
And congregate upon Roy's Corner.
I want provisions for a cruise!
I want some tins of Henizes' stews!
I want some bacon - want some bread
-
No, I'll take crispbread instead.
Where do I get paraffin?
Cut the ham up nice and thin!
Can I buy fishing tackle here?
Will you supply a case of beer?
Behold the crowd around the bars,
In sweaters, shorts and panamas!
What gaiety! What summer dresses!
What damsels, in what new distresses!
Stop Me, buy one, two or three,
Strawberry for you, vanilla for me;
Let's buy sun-glasses and a map,
A guide book, and a yachting cap,
Sunburn-lotion, films, and camera,
What glorious impedimenta!
Down to the Boatyards, and the Boat,
We'll eat our first meal here afloat!
The river's packed from dusk till
dawning,
From Wroxham Bridge right down to
Horning.
The sails are set, the wind is wanting,
Right, you lubbers! Start off quanting!
Ah, but there's wind on Wroxham
Broad;
Aye, and there's traffick. What a horde!
There's no right side and no wrong
side,
Just a weak side and a strong side;

Plough down dinghies when you're
merry,
But always give way to a wherry;
Gently, gently, with the paint
You might think it's tough. It ain't!
Remember, if you wouldn't bruise her,
That there's no brakes aboard a
cruiser,
And if the worst comes, in your
durance
Thank your stars that there's insurance.
The wise man spends his afternoon
On Wroxham Broad, for he knows soon
The breeze will drop, and leave his
mast sick
At Salhouse, or at Woodbastwick.
But what a change on Sunday morning!
Everybody's gone to Horning.

by Alan Hunter

THE NORFOLK PLAQUE & HISTORY.

1.

As you travel from your home to this fair county, have you ever wondered, when deep in thought, how it all began?

It is known that the Danes often ravaged these lands, and the dwellers often ran to the churches. However, that didn't save them as the Vikings used to burn these tapestries of faith.

The Vikings invaded Norfolk from the year 865 till 1066 when William the Conquer became King. Despite the new King, there were uprisings in Norwich and in 1272 thirteen members of a priory were murdered and those responsible for this grotesque crime were put to death publicly by hanging.

The inroads of the sea brought sailing vessels to Great Yarmouth, and with it a disastrous plaque. How it became as it did, even the history books of time cannot portray, except perhaps from the port they sailed from. An Angel occurred but not of scenic beauty, but a rodent, she was to arrive in a sailing vessel with goods to the newly formed Great Yarmouth.

People gathered on the formed quayside to welcome the sailing vessels in. Healthy people going about their business of the day, in the year 1348. When this ship docked, it was too late, the Angel of Death had arrived.

Her sailors were ill, and some were dead. This vessel had carved a deadly trade route from the Far East. People panicked, some fainted, they had to run to get away from this evil. In hours it spread along the river valleys and hamlets close to the breaches of Great Yarmouth.

Every day a new village, every day the angel spread her wings; swelling in the armpits and groin, fever, vomiting and diarrhoea. People could go to bed in the evening and by morning they were dead.

The Plaque was deadly in Yarmouth and 7,000 died. When it reached Norwich 50,000 would perish. Twenty days and night it would reign, people trying to flee its grasp, some running into the tall reeds trying to escape the contagiousness.

This disease showed no mercy and attacked the Norfolk peasantry with vengeance. Cattle stalls became contaminated hotbeds, the desolate swamps of the flatlands housed the dying, people fled to the monasteries hoping their seclusion would free them of this rat flea.

Village by village would be affected, cruelly children too, the magnitude was enormous.

From Binham in the East to Daws Heath in the West the plaque attacked.

It spread haphazardly across east to south leaving a wake of devastation behind.

Sometimes it would spread by road, sometimes by the newly forming rivers. People drawing water from these rivers would themselves become contaminated.
This sickness befell people everywhere, it was like black smoke, nowhere to hide or run, it killed within a week.

Great Yarmouth would be devastated. The point of origin, the crowded rows where opening one door you could almost touch the neighbour; two-thirds would perish here.

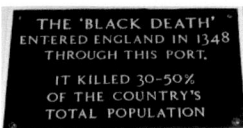

THE 'BLACK DEATH'
ENTERED ENGLAND IN 1348
THROUGH THIS PORT.

IT KILLED 30-50%
OF THE COUNTRY'S
TOTAL POPULATION

Houses within the area of contamination would be boarded up and markers put on doors. Some say the area is haunted, and at night a young screaming woman in a shawl and long dress is seen running towards the docks.

Fire was the only thing that would stop the Angel of Death which thrived in the overcrowded towns.

Strangely the plague disappeared almost as quickly as it started. The ship in the newly formed Great Yarmouth harbour was burned, everything with it turned to ashes.

In Norfolk and Suffolk 57,000 people would perish, and harvests rotted in the fields.

The animals that were left were devalued in price and peasants who survived wanted to pay to recoup the harvest if possible.

Through their perseverance they would be paid 4p a day to get the work done. The Black Death created discontent and famine as the poor became fed up with the rich, who had escaped most of the plague.

In retaliation, looting started in the countryside and anger become bloodshed. The authorities put in emergency legislation and implemented wage levels, making it a crime to refuse what is offered, it became unpopular and resulted in the peasant's revolt.

Nearer wetlands and with the Black Death still around, life had to go on.

The labour-intensive work of peat digging still had be worked. Peasant's revolt or not, the Monastery in Norwich burned 200,000 bales of peat a year.

The massive task to dig the peat to heat the large buildings took men hours, it was hard and unpleasant as the men had to dig deep for the compacted calorific block.

The industry of peat digging peaked in the 13th century as water from the sea was flooding, making digging more difficult. Where flooding wasn't so severe it was possible to cut, but the squelching of the hand tool against the block was back breaking work.

East Anglia was hard hit by the plaque and the next downturn to hit East Anglia was the decline of this precious fuel.

The peat cutting industry started to wane, the impact of the plaque on labour, the rise of sea levels, and dredging for wet peat blocks too dry and shape; all had a big impact.

Deep extraction was no longer possible, and the areas were left for the sea to devour and become what we know as the Broads.

The Church known as Norwich Priory from 1440 would no longer require peat for fuel as wood was becoming available.

The name Norfolk derives from 'Northern People,' and East Anglia derives from the Anglo-Saxon Kingdom of the East Angles.

The dialect of this county is rich and broad, but sadly not spoken as much today.

Many phrases have died away, but speech perhaps found in some little village by the old man of the home; sitting in his rocker with a long clay pipe, you might just hear Broad Norfolk. Although the rigours of the century may be present one might still here the term,

"Normal for Norfolk,"; alluding to the county's perceived status as 'quirky, rustic, and back water.'

To escape their world into ours and relive, and step back into a world long ago, a world that still opens it heart out to the visitor. Stories to tell, museums to visit, railways of yesteryear, wide stretches of marshland with their haunting stories.

Quiet dykes to sit and ponder, visit Great Yarmouth, and listen to the old folk telling of its rich fishing history; the barrels of herring that once stood on the now depleted dockside. Sail the rivers in genuine wooden boats of 'Swallows and Amazons'.

Enjoy the folk lore, the customs of the men on the marshes and the reed cutters work and stories. The gorgeous sunsets Norfolk has to offer sends shivers down your spine, tall grasses, bulrushes, reed field banks, spikes of purple loosestrife, willow herbs, and many scenes to allure you into this unforeseen quiet rural landscape of the past. May be on your journey through time you will see the Eel catcher, maybe see a Redshank or Lapwing, and perhaps the most beautiful sight, if quiet, the acrobatic antics of the little bearded Titmouse.

The wherry history, the transportation of material from source to village, these craft have stories to tell themselves, and are rich in history. If not a breath of wind, men would punt these long laden craft upriver to its destination or down river back to Great Yarmouth. The wherryman scans critically the reaches of the river ahead, he sees the changes and he's alert of time. He is aware of the silhouette in the whispering reed, it's an angler's boat, the only mysterious haunting noise he hears is the splash of the punt and the bows rippling through the solitude of the river of time.

The Vikings were close enough culturally to the Anglo-Saxons that they were able to integrate quickly. It is difficult to distinguish a genetic contribution, although many East Anglicans must have Viking ancestry. But they probably gave an extra stimulus to processes that might have happened anyway. Thetford grew to be 75 hectares in size and by the end of the period was smaller than Norwich. The Vikings have a reputation as merchants and it is known Danish traders resided in several towns, though regional and local exchange seems to have been more important than international. Most importantly, they helped in the unification of England and in the creation of the Norfolk people.

THE END

WROXHAM

The station was originally intended to be on the Wroxham side of the river, but a change of plan resulted in it being sited in Hoveton. However, it was misleadingly named 'Wroxham' station for many years.

WROXHAM STATION.

It was renamed 'Hoveton and Wroxham' during the mid-1960s but locals and regular visitors still refer to it by its old name.

Hoveton's large village store is dubbed 'the world's largest village store'. Alfred Roy opened his first store in Coltishall in 1895, with a second store opening in Hoveton in 1899; this store having since been modernised.

Boatbuilding in the Broads has existed for as long as the waters themselves.

One of the longest-established builders are the family firm of Landamores, based at Hoveton Their story began back in 1923 when the founder, Ted Landamore, opened a fledgling boat hire business. During subsequent years, he started to build small cruisers and water buses as his business grew.

By Booking direct you secure competitive prices
Send P.C. for Free Illustrated Catalogue

E. C. LANDAMORE & CO.
Hire Craft Specialists
WROXHAM, NORFOLK BROADS
Telephone : Wroxham 50
Telegrams : " Landamore, Wroxham "

Landamores acquired a reputation as first - class boatbuilders; its craftsmen creating some of the best-made vessels on the water.

But, as with most firms, the advent of World War II saw an abrupt change in direction as all hands were used for the war effort.

In 1942, the main building shop was extended to make room for the construction of two 65-foot RAF air-sea rescue launches. Between 1943 and the end of the war, 11 45-foot Admiralty Harbour launches were built.

The twin villages of Wroxham and Hoveton sitting either side of the River Bure are known as the 'capital of the Broads'.

Also sitting on the Hoveton side is one of the Broads' boatyards: Barnes Brinkcraft. Brian and Jill Thwaites bought Barnes Brinkcraft during the 1970s and developed the business, joined by their sons Daniel and Matthew in the late 80s, Sadly, Brian died in 1992.

Also, on the Hoveton side of the river was Royall's Boatyard, which enjoyed a well-earned reputation for impeccable service and impressively well-maintained boats.

It is now part of Barnes Brinkcraft. A further small boatyard on the Hoveton side was called 'George Smith'.

This boatyard maintained old wooden cruisers like Songster, sadly, time has marched on, and George Smith has faded with time.

Time constantly moves on, especially around Broadland, from the heady days when all the boats were made of wood to those now made from glass reinforced plastic (GRP).

However, wooden boats can still be seen belonging to private owners, who spend thousands of pounds maintaining tradition and history.

When you stand on Wroxham Bridge – a bridge that has also been drastically changed — think to yourself what stories it could tell if it were able to talk!

Wroxham Bridge was rebuilt in brick and stone in 1619, replacing a bridge built in 1576, which itself replaced an earlier — probably wooden — structure.

The stone for the current bridge came from St Benet's Abbey and the parapets bore a date from the 1890s. The brickwork could have come from Ruymps Brickworks , Sprowston.

Looking upriver, it's not hard to imagine life of yesteryear: the gently flowing river, carefree people in their summer clothes, and the peace there must have been sailing up and down on a boat .

Idyllic dreams , historical anecdotes , glimpses of wildlife and secrets of craft life; not forgetting 'the ole Norfolk boys' with their long clay pipes There is no place like the Norfolk Broads, no craft is as comfortable as a Broads boat, and there is no holiday like sailing or cruising there.

Our 'Norfolk boy,' John Kett, gives us the following to dwell upon We can't show yew
mount'n,
An, bor, we're short o' hills,
An 'yew oon't take long a' countin'
Ar castles an' ar mills.
But don't yew set there sighin'
Jus' east yar oyes. Up high
Where clouds an 'badd are flyin',
An 'see ar Norfick sky.

The only unpleasant side of living in Wroxham during the 30s and early 40s was the weekly visit of two men with their horse and trailer, known as 'the honey cart,' who had come to collect the waste from the outside toilets. There were tales of people still sitting on the toilet when the hatch would open, and the pail would be dragged out from under them, although I seem to recall that the men used to whistle loudly to warn you that they were on their way!

Forwarding on, In 1987 my wife and I moved to this fair county and my wife became a stewardess on one of the long wooden crafts offering Broads tours. It was initially known as the Norfolk Broads tour company which was established in 1935.

The boats were acquired from William Littleboy and George Smith and Sons.

In 1942 all boats had to be disabled in case East Anglia was invaded.

After the war years, people in the 1950s had more leisure time, and by 1959 new boats were acquired. They were 'Princess Anne' and 'Princess Alexandra'; both 52ft in length and licensed to carry 78 passengers. 'Dutchess built 1924 by Landamores too.

The owner, Charles Hanniford, who originally moved to Norfolk on health grounds, then changed the name to what it is known as today; 'Broads Tours.

All the Broads Crafts, had varnished hulls. They were very clean, had a toilet, and right at the back the tea Urn filled and ready for use.

Today the enchanting beauty, the rolling cloud and thanks to man removing by hand 900 million cubic feet of peat for heat, and the rising sea level that entered them centuries ago, now the broads had been formed, so as you sit and ponder the quiet radiance drinking your beverages one reflects in these times our tree of Life.

1969....The year it all started, the year my wife and I were to come on the Broads for a holiday but earlier it nearly didn't happen.

We had never heard of Norfolk or the Broads. I worked for London Transport, a good job on the underground doing early, middle, and late shifts. Life was tough but so enjoyable and a pleasure to go to work.

Chris my wife worked at a local shoe company in Sutton High Street in Surrey. We had been married for a year and lived in a upstairs flat in Sutton. It was only that my mother had invited us to Sunday dinner that the conversation started on a boating holiday.

I was naive! What's a boating holiday I said? Well, I was told by my stepfather rather abruptly, "It's what it says". I replied, 'But what is it?' Then the usual Sunday arguments started.

My stepfather was an arrogant man, thought he knew it all type? Mother though, calmed it down and out came the brochure. She said we are having this, it's called 'Salamander', look at this little boat, be ideal for you two, it was called 'Songster'.

I was hesitant, we both were, and I said to my mum, "I've never worked a boat, how does the thing," yes, thing I called it, "How does it work?"

My father then quipped, " You are thick", then another argument started. I finished by saying, "Yes but at least I do drive a tube train!" That shut him up, mum said, " Will you two stop it."

Mum said, "I will pay for it you will enjoy it." I was still hesitant, but I agreed. Going back to our flat I said to Chris, "Well I hope Mum is right, the following day I rang her and said "Ok but I haven't any transport and it's a long way isn't it?" She said, "Dad will take you," and again I replied, "Oh, what grumpy?" Mum was not amused.

The Saturday arrived and we got to Mum's home with our one suitcase packed, it was loaded, and we sat in the back of grumpy's motor, I called it a 'rolls canadly, rolls now one hill can hardly get up the next, an old black ford prefect. But looking out of the windows as Dad drove and Mum nattered, it was different.

I remember, this place called Norfolk was over 200 miles from where my Mother lived in Worcester Park. I looked at the vast expanse of fields; the greenery was stunning.

Eventually we got to Norfolk, and on the road from Norwich to Wroxham. It was pretty but I still thought of this boat; niggly little things. Eventually Dad said, " Now look we are almost here". He drove over the bridge, and I saw the wooden boats, and they looked nice, but they were still and not moving.

Arriving following an Atlas, we found George Smith's boatyard. I was amazed they were shiny and impressive but where was this so called 'thing' we were going to have?

We were told in a funny language, "Over tha bor." "Eh", I said to my wife, "they also speak funny, no wonder they are so far away, there is no civilisation!" "Shhh", she said, "Don't start!"

Yes, I know readers even then all those years ago it's best to keep one's lips sealed especially in strange places.

We had been on the boat for about 30 mins when a voice said, " Are you ready for a trial run!" I didn't know what that was, this little chap climbed aboard and said, " My name is

Sonny (that name was to become a friend as the years went by)."

"Let me show you everything sir". Well, he did, and I was amazed, all this on a little boat like Songster; a 24ft long piece of wood by8ft high. I said, " but where's the bed. Chrissy said 'that's all you think about' my face went red.

Then came that time he said, "Ok let's start". Turning the key, the little engine fired up, I again said, "How do I stop this in motion?" He replied, "All will be revealed don't worry."

Don't worry, that was the first thing going round my head! He got off, undid the front rope, and cast it on the side then went to the back undid that and got back on.

We were afloat, he stood in front of the control panel and got hold of this shaft and pushed it forward, fiddled about with a lever and slowly we went forward.

Again, in this strange language he said, "Tha ya go Bor easy." I looked at Chris and sort of gulped! "Nah you take it back it's not for me."

Reluctantly he took her back to the yard. I watched him do it so easily, even mooring up.

So, we were back at the yard facing the way we had come. I said to Chris, "I'm going to see Mum," She said, "What for we got to have it now it's been paid for."

I turned and said a few strong words, but we stayed. I think Chris then went to the shop for food for a couple days.

Putting the canopy up and then the plastic sides came down and I had to go and put the couplings together to make it watertight. The first night wasn't to be the best. I found the old boat to be draughty but liveable. Unbeknown to me at the time, she was to be the start of my Norfolk Life.

Chris, bless her, had made me a cup of tea and it did taste nice, and she sat beside me, and we were contented. Little Songster was rubbing her magic and we were three. I just took it all in and the smell, it was so fresh as it is now with the tall expanse of trees going towards Horning was vividly enchanting.

I knew this because we had a little map brought from Roy's.
Soon these majestic trees opened, and we were heading towards our first stop; to our left were lovely little homes set close to the river with some majestically cut lawns.

Then my nightmare loomed as white sails, the one thing I was fretting about (wooden craft known as yachts) were zigzagging across the water in front. had to slow right down on a strange little floating home, but it was as though baby Songster was telling me how to do it.

We had a couple of near scrapes with vocabulary unprintable, but we got through!

The Swan pub was a beckoning sight, we moored clumlisy but we got a spot, sealing out wooden home up, and the wooden key fob in my pockets,we went in and ordered a lovely pint of ale and Chris had lager and we sat there and had a good chat and even my lovely wife agreed it was nice and she said, "I'm glad you stayed, this is so enjoyable away from the crowds we endure." She was right, the atmosphere was different.

So, this was how we arrived in Norfolk and that little boat. We enjoyed mooring in dykes in the most remarkable villages, villages you only ever read about in library books.

We met lovely people but looming on the horizon was our nightmare; returning the boats.

When I got to the dyke on that horrible Saturday morning, I stood proud in Baby Songster's well and with a craftsman voice I said to her, "Let's show them what we can do!" Eyes from the yard watched and Baby Songster didn't let me down, she glided into an allotted space, we very gently nudged her stern and Sonny was watching and waiting as we were the last boat in.

When she was tied up I turned off her little engine and, yes, with tears in my young eyes I gently kissed her and said, "Thank you for an enjoyable week."

"Little Songster" was always in my mind, even today as I re write this story. Sadly, now she doesn't exist, a little boat with a Morris Vendetta engine brought us happiness.

I wouldn't change it for the world although I can't talk much 'bor' of this funny old language

they call 'Norfolk Dialect'! I will, in my heart, remember that little 24ft x8ft wooden home called 'Songster", in George Smith's yard in 1969 with Sonny the yardman showing me where she lay waiting.

After holidaying in Norfolk from 1969 to 1987, we moved here in 1987 and for the last 32 years have been able to call this beautiful place our 'home'. And so, readers, this is my introduction to Norfolk's fair County and the beautiful Norfolk Broads and Songster, my guardian Angel.

THE END

David even designs his own front covers,everything about JDBBooklets is made by David, his early schooling and his love of art shows when he designs covers, colours are important, and this is portrayed in this time frame. If photos are by photographers David always writes to get permission. The above portays the beauty of Norfolk in an way of enticement to this alluring county, the very county David loves writing about he say in the Norfolk tounge. 'Wuss a matter, owld partner my Chrissy say?I say bin eertin thart new-fangled tinned muck and im a sufferin with a belly-eerk. So Ise say "keep a troshin ole partner'. Norfolk the dialect that makes this county bootiful, and David even put poems in his books, no other author mixes verse with story. So if he isnt designing hes writing,David is a talented man trying to raise monies for charity, the MNDA which he is an official fund raiser and to date has raised by books alone £2557.27 Please support him if you can his wonderful website is www.jdbbooklets.org.uk

Norfolk Railways.
1.

This is the night mail crossing the Border,
Bringing the cheque and the postal order,

Letters for the rich, letters for the poor,
The shop at the corner, the girl next door.

Pulling up Beattock, a steady climb:
The gradient's against her, but she's on time.

Past cotton-grass and moorland boulder
Shovelling white steam over her shoulder,

Snorting noisily as she passes
Silent miles of wind-bent grasses.

Birds turn their heads as she approaches,
Stare from bushes at her blank-faced coaches.

Sheep-dogs cannot turn her course;
They slumber on with paws across.

In the farm she passes no one wakes,
But a jug in a bedroom gently shakes.

Dawn freshens, Her climb is done.
Down towards Glasgow she descends,
Towards the steam tugs yelping down a glade of cranes
Towards the fields of apparatus, the furnaces
Set on the dark plain like gigantic chessmen.
All Scotland waits for her:
In dark glens, beside pale-green lochs
Men long for news.

Letters of thanks, letters from banks,
Letters of joy from girl and boy,
Receipted bills and invitations
To inspect new stock or to visit relations,
And applications for situations,
And timid lovers' declarations,
And gossip, gossip from all the nations,
News circumstantial, news financial,
Letters with holiday snaps to enlarge in,
Letters with faces scrawled on the margin,
Letters from uncles, cousins, and aunts,
Letters to Scotland from the South of France,
Letters of condolence to Highlands and Lowlands
Written on paper of every hue,
The pink, the violet, the white and the blue,
The chatty, the catty, the boring, the adoring,
The cold and official and the heart's outpouring,
Clever, stupid, short and long,
The typed and the printed and the spelt all wrong.

Thousands are still asleep,
Dreaming of terrifying monsters
Or of friendly tea beside the band in Cranston's or Crawford's:

Asleep in working Glasgow, asleep in well-set Edinburgh,
Asleep in granite Aberdeen,
They continue their dreams,
But shall wake soon and hope for letters,
And none will hear the postman's knock
Without a quickening of the heart,
For who can bear to feel himself forgotten?

Memories of steam, its rich heyday, and **Norfolk's Poppy line,** our journey starts as your author was a signalman in Surrey a nineteen-year-old, many memories and knowledge but we are in Norfolk so let us travel on the lines that use steam still starting with the North Norfolk.

The poppy line got its name from Poppy Land' a term that was coined in the 19th Century by the poet and theatre critic Clement Scott and generally refers to the section of the North Norfolk coast. Regular passenger operation began on 1 May 1844 with a passenger service of seven trains each way. After a suspension of work, the Holt to Cromer section of line was completed by direct labour and opened on 16 June 1887.

A through Kings Cross to Cromer express started running in August 1887, and although the construction had been expensive, the boost to revenue from the new line was considerable. A second train was put on the following year, in the down direction consisting of coaches slipped at Peterborough from a GNR Manchester train. The time from Kings Cross to Cromer was typically 4+1⁄2 hours, but the GER did Liverpool Street to Cromer in 3+1⁄2 hours.

The Eastern and Midlands Railway was formed in 1881 by the amalgamation of several

small railways in the Isle of Ely, Cambridgeshire, Lincolnshire and Norfolk, England, including the Yarmouth and North Norfolk Railway, the Lynn and Fakenham Railway and the Yarmouth Union Railway. Many of these lines were built by contractors Wilkinson and Jarvis. In 1903 a station was added at Weybourne, having previously been refused. Weybourne railway station is preserved by the North Norfolk Railway. It was formerly part of the Midland and Great Northern Joint Railway route between Melton Constable and Cromer.

Under the Railways Act 1921, the line, along with the rest of the M&GN, was jointly managed by the LMS and LNER, retaining its own directors and staff. This continued until 1935, when the parent companies agreed that local administration should be undertaken by the LNER. The line became part of the Eastern Region of British Railways under the Transport Act 1947.

In May 1973, the railway was the scene of filming for the episode "The Royal Train" of the popular TV programme Dad's Army. In 2001 it was announced that the railway was in danger of closure, due to the landlords of Sheringham station reportedly wanting to sell the site for redevelopment, and the railway's lease on the site expiring in June of that year.

The railway was able to raise £290,000 to purchase the site, but it was saved by public donations and members of the public operate the trains, with the awards we finish-
NRHA: The National Rail Heritage Awards Volunteers Award, for Holt signal box.
2009 - NHRA: The Invensis Rail Signalling Award: Structure, Holt signal box
2016 - Hoseasons Tourism Awards: Best 'large attraction' in Norfolk and Suffolk
2016 - Heritage Railway Association: Annual Award (Large Groups), for extending steam services of the main line between two major coastal resorts and extending the boundaries of railway preservation
2018 - Heritage Railway Association: Coiley Locomotive Engineering Award, Runner-up, for 90775 major overhaul.

Our next railway is at **Dereham the mid Norfolk railway**. The King's Lynn line was originally operated by the Lynn & Dereham Railway, The Eastern Counties Railway (ECR) was an English railway company incorporated in 1836 intended to link London with Ipswich via Colchester, and then extend to Norwich and Yarmouth. The Lynn and Dereham Railway and the Norfolk Railway both obtained Parliament's permission to build lines to

Dereham in 1845, at the height of the so-called "Railway Mania", when railways were being frantically built across the whole country.

In 1857 the line between Dereham and Wells opened. In 1857 the line between Dereham and Wells opened. The Wells & Fakenham Railway, later part of the Great Eastern Railway's Wymondham to Wells branch and became a junction in 1866 with the arrival of the West Norfolk Junction Railway.

The West Norfolk Junction Railway was the next to come to Wells, on 17 August 1866.

The line came from Heacham on an 18+1/2-mile single track aimed at exploiting the great arc of coastline between Hunstanton and Yarmouth.

This line entered Wells on a sharp curve, turning through a full 180 degrees before converging with the Wells & Fakenham branch from Dereham for the final approach.

West Norfolk services used the outer face of a sheltered wooden island platform to the south of the station, with the inner face for services to Dereham and Wymondham.

Although the original four signal boxes at Dereham have been demolished, two of the boxes have been rebuilt since the preservation of the site.

The original Dereham North box is preserved close to the village of Hindolveston.

The Mid-Norfolk Railway (MNR) is a 171/2 miles preserved standard gauge heritage railway, one of the longest in Great Britain.

Mid-Norfolk Railway Operated by Mid-Norfolk Railway Preservation Trust it has 5 Stations and its entire Length is 17 miles with 15 miles operational. The Mid-Norfolk Railway is the longest standard-gauge heritage railway in East Anglia and runs through the Heart of Norfolk.

The railway has its headquarters in Dereham and runs south to Wymondham Abbey Halt station.

The Mid-Norfolk Railway Preservation Trust was set up in 1995 to buy the line from Wymondham to Dereham.

Yaxham became the centre of operations, and permission was given to clear the line of undergrowth and to build a platform to run trains.

The station at Dereham was cleaned up, and open days held. Since then, the MNR has restored Dereham Station to its former glory, and installed run-round loops at Dereham, Wymondham and more recently Thuxton with a fully operational signal box.

The line between Dereham to Worthing has also been reopened to passenger trains.

Exceptionally if you want to enjoy the greenery and sample Norfolk Fayre, you will enjoy fayre like Locally baked scones, clotted cream, fresh strawberries, and tea, all served on fine Norfolk bone china during a scenic 11-mile journey through the Heart of Norfolk countryside.

Or you can simply digest Fresh finger sandwiches, locally baked scones and a selection of delicious cakes are all served up on elegant three-tier stands by smartly attired staff.

Indulge in a true British favourite, smartly served up on our steam train, travel in style enjoy the romantic days of the past.

Or if recently married a unique and different atmosphere awaits you with a thrill of the past imagine arriving by a vintage bus or a coach- and the charm of a where your own 'private train' will pull in to take you and your guests gently through the delightful countryside to enjoy your very special wedding breakfast on board ... a wonderfully unique experience for you and your guests to treasure forever.

As with the Poppy line why not Climb aboard the footplate of a steam locomotive or in the cab of a diesel. Join our crews for an exciting journey, This is a fantastic way to view the

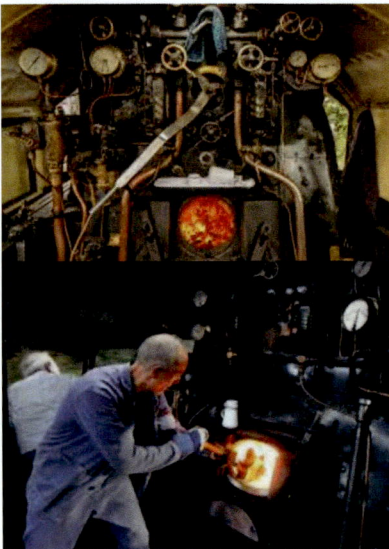

life of a driver's day on the railway, whilst taking in the thrill of sights and sounds and life on the footplate like in the cab, and feeling the heat of the fire and if lucky being served bacon and eggs on the fireman's shovel

Ride the footplate of the majestic 80078 locomotive, help put water in the tank of the little 9466 locomotive, or if allowed step on board the majestic Lion of South Africa 60009. The mid Norfolk railway has it all . This rich historical railway from Dereham, the stations south to Wymondham Abbey are Yaxham, Thuxton, Hardingham and Kimberley Park, are all being tastefully restored and retain many original features. To the north of Dereham, we are restoring the line through North Elmham and terminating at the County School station.

As of Wroxham we are at Wells first and the little railway to **Walsingham, Wells Station** is clearly signposted on the Stiffkey Road just to the east of Wells-next-the-Sea. The Wells Walsingham Light Railway, a delightful narrow-gauge line which covers more than four miles from Wells-next-the-Sea to Walsingham in Norfolk. Enjoy a half-hour trip through beautiful countryside whilst you take in the evocative sights, sounds, and smells of steam travel. Your unforgettable trip back in time clanks over and under bridges, chuffs past a hillfort and through a real ghost platform. Plus, the driver of the loco called has seen clearly

through the loco window a face!. During this time the number of what staff refer to as "happenings" have been numerous. Everything from things going missing and re-appearing to spectral figures crossing the line or peering out of the signal box window has been witnessed.

The current line starts at Wells station, on the A149 coast road just south of the town. After leaving the station trains begin to climb the 1 in 80 gradients to Warham, passing the remains of the Leicester Lime Works and The Midden Halt, a small request stop station serving a camp site, before passing under a road bridge carrying the Wells to Walsingham road.

At Warham the line starts to descend and passes over a level crossing before reaching the request stop at Warham station.

Leaving the station the line passes through a cutting, and under a road bridge (the site of Wighton Station from 1982 to 2005), then over an embankment close to the Warham Camp hill fort, before reaching the original and current Wighton station, which was

temporarily renamed Seton's Halt between 1982 and 2005. In 1986 two larger locomotives were built, entering service for the 1987 season; these were the new 2-6-0+0-6-2 Garratt locomotive No 3 Norfolk Hero and the Bo-Bo diesel locomotive No 4 Norfolk Harvester.

Leaving this little railway, we join the next steam trip at **Wroxham Norfolk's longest narrow-gauge railway which runs between the historic market town of Aylsham and bustling town of Wroxham,** the heart of the Norfolk Broads. The East Norfolk Railway Act of 1864 included plans for an extension to Aylsham. The formal Act of Parliament to extend to Aylsham was not granted until 16th April 1876.

The Railway is built on the track bed of the former Great Eastern Railway between Wroxham and Aylsham. Originally opened in 1880 the line survived for passenger traffic until 1952, eleven years before the infamous Beeching Cuts ! Today we have a collection of some of the largest and most powerful 15-inch gauge steam locomotives ever built,

The Bure Valley Railway is a major tourist attraction, so why not treat yourself and ride the line to wroxham or the beautiful village of aylsham.

Aylsham is a historic market town and civil parish on the River Bure in north Norfolk, England. The river rises near Melton Constable, 11 miles upstream from Aylsham and continues to Great Yarmouth and the North Sea

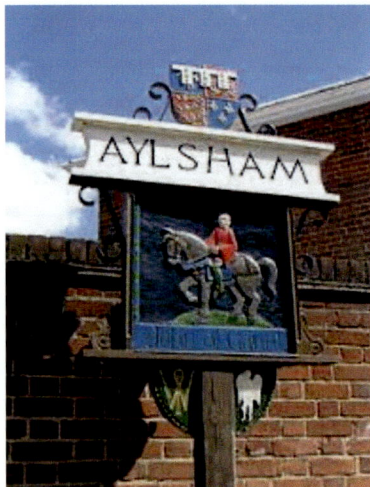

The town is close to large estates and grand country houses at Blickling, Felbrigg, Mannington and Wolterton, which are important tourist attractions. Archaeological evidence shows that the site of the town has been occupied since prehistoric times. Aylsham is just over two miles from a substantial Roman settlement at Brampton, linked to Venta Icenorum at Caistor St Edmund, south of Norwich, by a Roman road which can still be traced in places – that site was a bustling industrial centre with maritime links to the rest of the empire. Excavations in the 1970s provided evidence of several kilns, showing that this was an industrial centre, pottery and metal items being the main items manufactured.

Aylsham once had two railway stations, both now closed, Aylsham South railway station (on the Great Eastern line between County School railway station, near North Elmham and Wroxham) and the Aylsham North railway station.

Aylsham, Norfolk on the Midland and Great Northern Joint Railway line from the Midlands to the Norfolk Coast, it was closed in 1959 along with the rest of the line. It was demolished following the closure and is now a car park for the Weavers Way footpath.

Aylsham South railway station served the town of Aylsham in Norfolk from 1880 to 1981.

The period station buildings were subsequently demolished in 1989.

A railway line was opened as part of the Norfolk Railway's extension from East Dereham to Fakenham in 1849, and to Wells by 1857.

County School railway station was built by the Great Eastern Railway in 1886 to serve the private school from which it took its name and following the completion of the East Norfolk Railway's branch line from Wroxham and Aylsham in 1882.

In 1903 the Norfolk County School became the Watts Naval School, although the station name remained unchanged. On 20 January 1915, the junction with the line to Aylsham and Wroxham was the site of an accident between a passenger train from Wells and a goods train from Foulsham. The responsibility for the crash was placed on the driver of the goods train, for failing to observe that his signals were at danger.

Aylsham is also the terminus for the Bure Valley Railway (on the site of Aylsham South railway station).

The Bure Valley Railway is a 15 in minimum gauge heritage railway which runs from Wroxham to Aylsham (9 miles) and is Norfolk's longest railway of less than standard gauge. Standard-gauge railway is a railway with a track gauge of (4 ft 8+1/2 in).

The standard gauge is also called Stephenson gauge (after George Stephenson), International gauge). Stephenson's Stockton and Darlington railway (S&DR) was built primarily to transport coal from mines near Shildon to the port at Stockton-on-Tees.

The initial gauge of 4 ft 8 in was set to accommodate the existing gauge of hundreds of horse-drawn chaldron wagons that were already in use on the wagonways in the mines.

The railway used this gauge for 15 years before a change was made to the (4 ft 8+1/2 in) in gauge.

So, there you have it folks a brief look at the trains of yesterday, trains and drivers that done everything and at the end of the day, nothing better than enjoying bacon and egg cooked on a shovel and a mug of tea sipped from a billy can ,water from the engine's boiler.

Letters of thanks, letters from banks,
Letters of joy from girl and boy,
Receipted bills and invitations
To inspect new stock or to visit relations,
And applications for situations,
And timid lovers' declarations,
And gossip, gossip from all the nations,
News circumstantial, news financial,
Letters with holiday snaps to enlarge in,
Letters with faces scrawled on the margin,
Letters from uncles, cousins, and aunts,
Letters to Scotland from the South of France,
Letters of condolence to Highlands and Lowlands
Written on paper of every hue,
The pink, the violet, the white and the blue,
The chatty, the catty, the boring, the adoring,

9.

The cold and official and the heart's outpouring,
Clever, stupid, short and long,
The typed and the printed and the spelt all wrong.

Thousands are still asleep,
Dreaming of terrifying monsters
Or of friendly tea beside the band in Cranston's or Crawford's:

Asleep in working Glasgow, asleep in well-set Edinburgh,
Asleep in granite Aberdeen,
They continue their dreams,
But shall wake soon and hope for letters,
And none will hear the postman's knock
Without a quickening of the heart,
For who can bear to feel himself forgotten?

My thanks to : *Nightborder by allpoetry.com.*
nnrailway.co.uk railway information & photos.
Wphen.org.uk Midland North Railway.
Walsingham Wells Railway.
Wikiwand.net Countrysude School Railway Photograph.
Magip.net Standard Gauge.
railwaytouring.net Steam trains.

THE END.

We in our time when visiting Norfolk have always seen on the lowlands beautiful windmills, well here is some history about these magnificent structures of the time.

Aslacton, Aslacton Mill was probably built in 1834, although there was a mill in Aslacton as early as 1751. Benjamin Gibson is the first recorded miller, and Barnabas Burroughes owned the mill from 1872 until his death on 18 December 1899. The mill passed to his widow, and after her death on 4 August 1903the mill was offered for sale by auction at the Railway Inn, Tivetshall on 25 August 1903.

Aylsham Cawston Road Mill was built in 1826 for Henry Soame. He died in 1833, and the mill passed to his son George. He ran the mill for several years before leasing it out. Miller John Neech became bankrupt in 1860, and George Soame took over the mill again. The mill was sold by auction on 18 June 1864 at the Dog Inn, Aylsham. A 6 horsepower (4.5 kW) steam engine had been installed to supply auxiliary power.

Billingford. Billingford Windmill is a grade II* listed brick tower mill at Billingford near Diss, Norfolk, England, which has been preserved and restored to working order. As of June 2009, the mill is under repair, with new sails being made. On 2–3 January 1976, the fantail was destroyed in a gale. A replacement was made and fitted in March 1976 by Messrs Barrett and Lawn, millwrights. On 14 July 1977, a 52 feet long fabricated steel stock was fitted by Lennard and Lawn, replacing a Columbian pine stock fitted when the mill was restored in 1962. In 1998, Norfolk Windmills Trust had the mill put back into complete working order.

Blakeney Tower Windmill, built-in 1769 is located on Friar Farm just to the east of the village of Blakeney in the English county of Norfolk The mill, which today is owned by the National Trust, stands in a static caravan site. The building has been evaluated for its historical interest as a Grade II listed building. The tower mill stands over four storeys and is 32 feet tall. The mill was powered with standard sails and a tailpole in its working days. The configuration powered two pairs of grindstones. The doors and windows are unusual in that they have Gothic arches, probably installed during rebuilding work in the 1800s. Also, during this period, four patent double-shuttered sails were installed.

Burnham Overy. The watermill was built in 1737; this date is recorded on the watermill. As initially created, it was a two-storey mill. Thomas Beeston was the miller in 1802. The windmill was built in 1814 and bore a tablet inscribed T. B. 1814 PEACE, referring to the banishment of Napoleon to Elba in that year. The watermill was probably raised by a storey at this date. The mills were offered for sale at the Norfolk Hotel, Norwich, on 3 August 1825. The windmill was described as having five floors, and the Patent sails had shutters made of copper. Union Mills or Roy's Mills are a Grade II listed combined tower mill and watermill at Burnham Overy, Norfolk, England, converted to residential accommodation.

Burnham Overy Staithe. Burnham Overy Staithe Windmill is a Grade II* listed building tower mill at Burnham Overy Staithe, Norfolk, England, converted to holiday accommodation. John Savory worked the mill until his death on 27 September 1863, and the mill passed to his son, also named John. In 1869, a law was passed that all trade horses should be licensed. John Savory was convicted in 1870 and fined £5 for having one more horse than he held a licence for. He was again convicted in 1873 and fined £5 for the same offence. The mill was sold by auction on 23 June 1888 at the Norfolk Hotel, Norwich. The premises comprise a steam mill powered by a 16 horsepower (12 kW) steam engine driving four pairs of millstones, the watermill driving three pairs of millstones and the windmill also driving three pairs of millstones.

Carbrooke. Mill Lane Mill is a Grade II listed tower mill at Carbrooke, Norfolk, England, conserved with some remaining machinery. Mill Lane Mill was built in 1856, replacing a post mill standing in 1811. The mill was built for Richard Dewing of Carbrooke Hall. Dewing died on 22 November 1876, and Edward May Dewing managed the estate. A steam engine had been installed as auxiliary power by 1888, driving a separate pair of millstones. The mill was offered for sale by auction on 30 July 1900 at the Mart, London EC. It was bought by Herbert Jeremiah Minns, who was the sitting tenant. The mill was part freehold and part copyhold. A pair of sails from Little Cressingham was fitted in 1920. Minns died on 16 August 1921, and the mill passed to his son Herbert Willie Minns.

Caston. Caston Tower Windmill is a grade II*listed tower mill at Caston, Norfolk, England, which is under restoration. The mill is also a scheduled monument. Caston Windmill was built in 1864, replacing a post mill standing in 1834. The tower was built by William Wright, a local builder, and fitted out by millwright Robert Hambling of East Dereham. It bears a date stone inscribed EW 1864, referring to Edward Wyer, who had owned the post mill. The mill caught fire during a storm on 24 March 1895, but the damage was not recorded. The Watton fire brigade was called upon to deal with the fire. Edward Wyer ran the mill until his death on 5 July 1897. His property was sold by auction on 7 October 1897 at the Dukes Head public house, Caston, but remained unsold. Wyer's son James took the mill and ran it until 1910, when he retired.

Catfield. Swim Coots Mill is a tower mill at Catfield, Norfolk, England, conserved with some remaining machinery. Swim Coots Mill was built in the early nineteenth century. It was marked on the 1838 Ordnance Survey map. The mill was working until at least the 1930s but was derelict by 1978. The mill has since been conserved, with the tower roofed over. Swim Coots mill is a two-storey tower mill that formerly had a boat-shaped cap winded by a fantail. It had four double Patent sails.

The tower is 15 feet in diameter at the base and 19 feet high to curb level. It drove a 5 feet 2 inches diameter scoopwheel housed internally. The mill also operated a single pair of millstones.

Cley. Cley Windmill is a grade II* listed tower mill at Cley next the Sea, Norfolk, England, converted to residential accommodation. Cley windmill was built in the early 19th century. It was not marked on William Faden's map of Norfolk published in 1797. The first mention was an advert in the Norfolk Chronicle of 26 June 1819, where the mill was for sale, described as "newly erected" and in the ownership of the Farthing family. The mill was not sold and remained the property of the Farthing family until 1875, when Dorothy Farthing, the then owner, died. The miller, Stephen Barnabas Burroughes, bought the mill. The Burroughes family worked it until c. 1912 when the business was transferred to their windmill at Holt.

Denver. Denver Windmill is a Grade II* listed tower mill at Denver, Norfolk, England; Denver windmill was built in 1835, replacing an earlier post mill marked on the 1824 Ordnance Survey map. The mill was built for John Porter, and the tower bears a datestone with the legend JMP 1835. A steam mill had been erected at the Denver windmill by 1863, powered by a 12 horsepower (8.9 kW) engine. This drove three pairs of millstones, as did the windmill.

Diss. Jay's Mill, Button's Mill or Victoria Road Mill is a tower mill at Diss, Norfolk, England, truncated and converted to residential accommodation. Button's Mill was built in c1817 on what was then Diss Common for Thomas Jay, who had purchased the mill's land in that year. Jay also owned a post mill at Stuston Road. The mill was built with eight sails, but these were blown off on 28 November 1836. Jay's post mill at Stuston Road had been blown down in a gale four days earlier. Millwright Henry Rush repaired the tower mill but only sported four sails; a replacement post mill was also built. Thomas Jay died on 3 April 1847, and the mill was run by his widow Sarah. It was offered for sale by auction on 5 September 1853 at the King's Head Hotel, Diss but remained unsold. It was again offered for sale October in 1856 and purchased by Michael Hawes. He was succeeded by William Hawes, who retired in 1880.

East Dereham. Norwich Road Mill or Fendick's Mill is a Grade II listed tower mill at East Dereham, Norfolk, England, which was most recently restored and reopened to visitors in 2013. Norwich Road Mill was built in 1836 by millwright James Hardy of Toftwood for Michael Hardy, who had a smock mill at Bittering. Hardy worked the mill himself but advertised it to let in 1837. John Armes took it. In 1877, Hardy was in financial difficulties, and the mill was sold by auction at the King's Arms Inn, East Dereham on 16 February 1844 and others at Gressenhall, Ovington and Wicklewood. The mill was bought for £650 by William Fendick. He had a post mill at West End, Shipdham. The mill was let to John Willden from 1850 to 1856. In 1863, William

Fendick died, and the mill was offered to let. The business was carried on by Fendick's widow Sarah until 1871, when their son William took over. A steam engine was installed as auxiliary power. He worked the mill until he died in 1904. The mill passed to his son William, running a tower mill at Mill Street, Mattishall. The mill was sold in 1909 to Charles Robert Gray and Arthur James Milk. Gray died in 1922. The sails were removed about this time, and a paraffin engine replaced the steam engine.

East Harling. Kenninghall Road Mill is a Grade II listed[1] tower mill at East Harling, Norfolk, England, converted to residential accommodation. The mill was probably built-in 1820. It first appeared in the Land Tax records that year, owned by Thomas Burlingham. The mill was sold by auction on 8 August 1943 at the Swan Inn, East Harling. Thomas Jary was the tenant miller at the time. James Lawrence had taken the mill by 1850. The mill was again offered by auction on 11 February 1854 at the Swan Inn. James Lawrence retired in 1875, and the mill was taken by his son Thomas He employed two brothers by the name of Pattinson, who was at the mill by 1902.[In 1912, Thomas Lawrence committed suicide in the mill, hanging himself.

East Runton. East Runton Windmill is a grade II listed tower mill at East Runton, Norfolk, England, converted to residential accommodation. The first record of this windmill is its appearance on Bryant's map of Norfolk, published in 1826. The mill was owned by Joseph Baker in 1836. He was a miller and brickmaker. The mill was to be let in 1843. On 1 November 1860, a girl was struck by one of the sails and knocked unconscious. The mill was working until at least 1908, when Ronald Hall was the miller, but it was derelict in 1926.

East Wretham. East Wretham Mill is a tower mill at East Wretham, Norfolk, England, converted to residential accommodation. East Wretham Mill was first mentioned in an advert in 1875 when it was described as "newly erected". A mill had been marked on the site in 1826 when it appeared on Bryant's map. Millers are recorded at this mill up to 1872. Edmund Land was the miller in 1878; having previously been at Stow Bedon smock mill Walter Weggett was the next miller Walter Littleproud followed him in 1883.

Frettenham. Frettenham Mill is a Grade II listed tower mill at Frettenham, Norfolk, England, converted to residential accommodation. Frettenham Mill was built in c1880 for Joshua Harper. He died in 1891, and the mill was offered for sale by auction at the Royal Hotel, Norwich, on 18 July 1891. It was bought by Alfred Herne, who worked it until c.1900.

Garboldisham. Garboldisham Mill is a Grade II* listed post mill at Garboldisham, Norfolk, restored. Although millers were recorded in Garboldisham during the Sixteenth Century, the first record of a windmill was in 1739 when Ishmael Pizzey left his windmill to his wife. In the 1770s, James Turner, a Blo' Norton farmer, built the surviving mill and was marked on Joseph Hodskinson's map of Suffolk, 1783 and Faden's map of Norfolk, 1797. Also shown on this map was a smock mill to the south, erected by James Turner in 1788.

Gayton. Gayton Mill is a Grade II listed tower mill at Gayton, Norfolk, England, truncated and converted to holiday accommodation. A post mill was standing at Gayton in 1797 when it was marked on Faden's map of Norfolk. The mill was advertised for sale in 1815 and 1819. The tower mill had been built by 1824 when it was marked on the first edition Ordnance Survey map of Norfolk. Robert Matthews was the miller in 1836. In 1872, the mill was offered to let. A steam mill powered by an eight horsepower (6.0 kW) Clayton & Shuttleworth steam engine was working an additional three pairs of French Burr millstones.

Great Bircham. Great Bircham Windmill is a Grade II listed tower mill in Great Bircham, Norfolk, England. The earliest record of a windmill in Great Bircham was in 1761 when miller Richard Miller made his will. The mill, probably a post mill, was offered for sale in 1769. In 1800 the miller, Robert Sparham, was in financial difficulties and made a Deed of Assignment. In 1804 the mill was offered for sale or let by George Humphrey. The next miller was Bloom Humphrey, followed by his widow Martha and then their son George. The mill remained in the Humphrey family until it was demolished in 1846 to enable a new tower mill to be built on its site.

Great Ellingham. Great Ellingham Windmill is a Grade II listed tower mill in Great Ellingham, Norfolk, England, converted to residential accommodation. Great Ellingham Mill was described as "newly erected" when advertised for sale by auction on 2 April 1849 at the Crown Inn, Great Ellingham. It was not sold and advertised for sale or to let in July 1849. The mill then had standard sails and drove a single pair of millstones. It was then five storeys tall.

Hickling tower mill was built in 1818 and had an eight-storey tarred tower that was substantially constructed with the brickwork of 30 inches thickness at the base. The building was 60 feet to the curb and 71 feet to the cap ridge. The mill stood back from the road, alone in a field. Unusually, for aesthetic reasons, the windows were all built one above the other, and in order not to detract from the overall strength of the tower, 13 of the 28 windows between the 1st and 7th floors were false.

Ludham High tower mill was an old mill having been built in 1742 to replace the Yarmouth_Road_postmill that had stood a few yards to the side. The mill stood next to the mill house, close to the village's east side road.

Old Buckenham, Old Buckenham Windmill is a tower flour mill that stands in Old Buckenham, Norfolk, England. It is a Grade II* listed building, notable for being the giant diameter windmill in the country. The tower was built in 1818 of brick in five storeys and is 8 meters (26.5 feet) in diameter at the base. The cap was boat-shaped and extended to the rear. At 7.3 meters (24 feet) in diameter, it was the largest known cap in the country, requiring five truck wheels and 17 centring wheels to carry the weight.

Potter Heigham tower windmill was built to replace an earlier post mill on or near the same site. The six-storey red brick 54-foot tower for Simon Boyce by the Suffolk millwrights, Martins, in 1849.

Reedham, Berney Arms Windmill is a tower mill located at Berney Arms alongside the River Yare at the south-western end of Breydon Water in the English county of Norfolk. The windmill is in an isolated spot in The Broads, around 3.5 miles (5.6 km) northeast of the village of Reedham and 4 miles southwest of Great Yarmouth. The mill has no road access but can be accessed by boat, foot, or Berney Arms railway station. It is a Scheduled Ancient Monument under the care of English Heritage. The windmill was built in 1865 for the Reedham Cement Company by the millwright firm of Stolworthy on the site of a previous mill. It was initially used to grind cement clinker, using chalk from Whitlingham near Norwich and clay dredged from Oulton Broad or Breydon Water, both brought to the mill by wherry. These materials were fired at nearby kilns. The kilns produced a clinker which was ground to a powder in the windmill. At this time, the cement works supported a small settlement with 11 inhabited houses. A chapel Cement production closed down in 1880. In 1883 the windmill was converted into a drainage mill to drain the surrounding marshland. The mill closed in 1948 when motor pumps replaced it. It was given to the Ministry of Works in 1951, and restoration began in 1967

St. Benet's Hulme or St. Bene't-at-Holme Abbey drainage mill was possibly built initially to crush cole (rape) seed to make colza oil for lamps before being converted to a drainage pump, the oldest tower mills in Norfolk and the oldest in the Broads. The mill was built with standard sails, but it had two traditional sails and two patent sails that turned clockwise in the latter stages of its life. Each patent sail had six bays of 3 shutters. The side pointed cap was horizontally boarded, and the stage was level with the abbey gateway.

Smallburgh tower windmill at Wayford Bridge was built as a four-storey drainage mill with a scoop wheel, but it also had a single pair of stones for grinding corn. In 1847, the millwrights Englands of Ludham, whose name is on the flood door. The single doored red brick tower was 30 feet high with a ground floor diameter of 15 feet with 18ins thick walls.

Sutton mill was built in 1789 with eight floors. When it was rebuilt after the fire of 1861, an additional floor was added, and patent sails replaced the standard sails. The nine-storey mill was topped by a traditional Norfolk boat shaped cap and had a gallery and petticoat.

By 2005, Sutton mill at 67' 6" was reputed to be the tallest remaining windmill in the county.

Thrigby, Thrigby Post Windmill is located in the civil parish of Mautby in the English county of Norfolk. The mill is on the south side of Mill Lane, 1,125 yards east of the village of Thrigby. The post mill is north of The River Bure, Breydon Water and the Halvergate Marshes. The post mill can be seen on the 1797 map of the area produced by Faden. The last miller of Thrigby was Alfred Hood, who was also a local farmer. He ran the mill until 1889, when the mill ceased working. In 1892 the wooden structure of the mill was found to be infested with death watch beetle and was then dismantled, leaving only the brick roundhouse.

West Winch Windmill is located in the village of West Winch in the English county of Norfolk. West Winch is two miles south of King's Lynn. The mill is a grade II listed building. The windmill was built in 1821 and is of brick construction, and the outside was tarred. The mill stands over five storeys with a gallery stage on the second floor. The windmill stopped production in 1936 and became derelict over the next 35 years.

Wymondham had a mill at an unknown location, presumably a post mill. 1702: Robert Sayer, miller 1808: George Hart, miller, bankrupt 1808: Stephen Buttolph, miller 1816: Stephen Buttolph, miller 1818: Stephen Buttolph died.

Weybourne Windmill is located on the eastern high ground above the village of Weybourne in the English county of Norfolk. On the northern side of the A149 coastal road that links King's Lynn to Great Yarmouth. The Windmill is 3 miles west of Sheringham and is within the Norfolk Coast. The mill is a grade II listed building. The Windmill was built in 1850 and consisted of five storeys constructed from red brick. The windmill ceased production in 1916 and fell into disrepair. In 1925 some restoration work of sorts took place, but as a result, most of the machinery was removed except for the windshaft.

William Critoph built the Yaxham tower mill in 1860. The 48 foot, the six-storey tarred tower had a ground diameter of 20 feet that narrowed by 2 feet per floor culminating with a horizontally boarded ogee cap with a six-bladed fan, a gallery and a ball finial that was still a garden ornament in the 1980s.

The four double shuttered sails, each with ten bays of 3 shutters, drove three underdriven stones, at least one pair of which were composite.

Standing in the heart of Norfolk's undulating fields, Bircham Windmill now looks as it did over 100 years ago. Around 300 mills ground corn for horse & cattle feed and bread-making in Norfolk.

Today, very few windmills are left, and Bircham Mill is considered one of the best remaining: it is the only windmill in working order in this area open to the public.

Great Bircham Mill is a five-storey tower mill with a stage at the third-floor level. The tower is 52 feet to curb level and 25 feet (outside diameter at the base), with 2 feet 6 inches thick walls. It has an ogee cap with a gallery.

A six-bladed fantail winds the cap. Four *double Patent sails* are carried on a cast-iron *windshaft*.

The *wallower* and *upright shaft* are made of cast iron.[

The *great spur wheel* has a cast-iron centre and iron teeth.

The mill drives two pairs of French Burr *millstones* tower mill was built for George Humphrey in 1846; a date stone to this effect is located between two windows on the first floor of the mill.

The mill was built from cream coloured bricks but was later tarred.

The mill was offered to let in 1856 and again in 1861.

In March 1864, George Humphrey was driving his cart whilst drunk, resulting in the death of his wife, Elizabeth.

In April, the mill was ordered to be sold by the mortgagees.

An auction was held on 13 May at the Hare Inn, Docking.

The next millers were Henry and Philip Stanton, followed by Walter Palmer.

He left Norfolk in 1882, and Joseph Wagg took the mill, followed by a succession of Howards.

William Howard was the last miller. The mill was working in 1916 but had ceased by 1922.

The sails and fantail had been removed by 1934

THE END

Norfolk Beauty

By
Malcolm Moulden

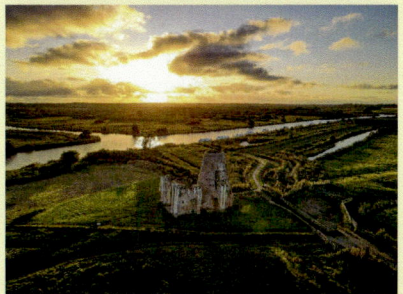

Local Girl Executed

Edith Cavell was born on 4 December 1865 in Swardeston, one of the earliest mentions of this place is in the Domesday book it is a village near Norwich. Her father was vicar for 45 years. She was the eldest of the four children of the Reverend Frederick Cavell (1824–1910) and his wife Louisa Sophia Warming (1835–1918). Edith's siblings were Florence Mary (b. 1867), Mary Lilian (b. 1870) and John Frederick Scott (1872–1923). Edith grew up and played like any youngster but was educated at Norwich High School for Girls. Norwich High School for Girls was founded in 1875 as the first GPDST school outside London.

Edith was then taught further at the boarding schools in Clevedon Somerset. It was run by nuns of the Community of the Sisters of the Church, an international body in the Anglican Communion living according to the Gospel values of poverty, chastity, and obedience. and Peterborough (Laurel Court).

She returned home to care for her father during a serious illness. The experience led her to become a nurse after her father's recovery. In April 1896, at the age of 30, Cavell applied to become a nurse probationer at the London Hospital under Matron Eva Luckes. Eva Abigail Charlotte Ellis Luckes was born in Exeter, Devon on 8 July 1854 into an upper-middle-class family. Her father, Henry Richard Luckes, was a banker who had established a comfortable home for his family in Newnham, Gloucestershire. Miss Luckes, the eldest of three daughters, was educated at Malvern, Cheltenham College and Dresden. She suffered from some physical disablement and had a horse to help her travel about the countryside. After finishing her education, she returned to Newnham and helped her mother run the house and visit the sick of the parish. It was this that developed her interest in nursing.

She worked in various hospitals in England, including Shoreditch The hospital was founded as the infirmary for St Leonard's Shoreditch Workhouse in 1777.

The workhouse was rebuilt between 1863 and 1866 and the infirmary was rebuilt in 1872. Edith Cavell served as Assistant Matron at the hospital from 1903 to 1906. It had become known as St Leonard's Hospital by 1920 and came under the management of London County Council in 1930.

It was the first hospital to receive casualties during the Blitz and then joined the National Health Service in 1948. (since renamed St Leonard's Hospital).

As a private travelling nurse, treating patients in their homes, Cavell travelled to tend patients with cancer, gout, pneumonia, pleurisy, eye issues and appendicitis. Edith Cavell was sent to assist with the typhoid outbreak in Maidstone during 1897.

Along with other staff she was awarded the Maidstone Medal.

In 1907, Edith Cavell was recruited by Dr Antoine Depage to be matron of a newly established nursing school, L'École Belge infirmaries Diplômées (or the Berkendael Medical Institute) on the Rue de la Culture (now Rue Franz Merjay), in Ixelles, Brussels.

In 1910, "Miss Cavell 'felt that the profession of nursing had gained sufficient foothold in Belgium to warrant the publishing of a professional journal' and, therefore, launched the nursing journal, L'infirmière".Within a year, she was training nurses for three hospitals, twenty-four schools, and thirteen kindergartens in Belgium.

When the First World War broke out, she was visiting her widowed mother in Norfolk.

She returned to Brussels, where her clinic and nursing school were taken over by the Red Cross.

With the outbreak of World War I, the ICRC found itself confronted with enormous challenges that it could handle only by working closely with the national Red Cross societies. Red Cross nurses from around the world, including the United States and Japan, came to support the medical services of the armed forces of the European countries involved in the war.

On 15 August 1914, immediately after the start of the war, the ICRC set up its International Prisoners-of-War (POW) Agency, which had about 1,200 mostly volunteer staff members by the end of 1914. By the end of the war, the Agency had transferred about 20 million letters and messages, 1.9 million parcels, and about 18 million Swiss francs in monetary donations to POWs of all affected countries.

In November 1914, after the German occupation of Brussels, Cavell began sheltering British soldiers and funnelling them out of occupied Belgium to the neutral Netherlands. Wounded British and French soldiers as well as Belgian and French civilians of military age were hidden from the Germans and provided with false papers by Prince Reginald de Croÿ at his château of Bellignies near Mons. From there, they were conducted by various guides to the houses of Cavell. This placed Cavell in violation of German military law. German authorities became increasingly suspicious of the nurse's actions, which were further fuelled by her outspokenness. She was arrested on 3 August

1915 and charged with harbouring Allied soldiers. She had been betrayed by Georges Gaston Quien, George Gaston Quien, a Frenchman who had defected to the German side in exchange for his release, disguised himself as an allied soldier in need of safe passage out of the country and made his way into the Clinique. He was communicated out in June, and throughout July the Clinique had an increasing number of German inspections and refugees that lacked well known passwords. However, The Germans had been suspicious of the Clinique for a long time, but lacked the hard evidence required to make arrests.

At her court-martial, she was prosecuted for aiding British and French soldiers, in addition to young Belgian men, to cross the Dutch border and eventually enter Britain. She admitted her guilt when she signed a statement the day before the trial. Cavell declared that the soldiers she had helped escape thanked her in writing when they arrived safely in Britain. This admission confirmed that Cavell had helped the soldiers navigate the Dutch frontier, but it also established that she helped them escape to a country at war with Germany who was later convicted by a French court as a collaborator.

She was held in Saint-Gilles prison for ten weeks, the last two of which were spent in solitary confinement. She made three depositions to the German police (on 8, 18 and 22 August), admitting that she had been instrumental in conveying about 60 British and 15 French soldiers, as well as about 100 French and Belgian civilians of military age, to the frontier and had sheltered most of them in her house. The penalty, according to German military law, was death. Paragraph 58 of the German Military Code determined that "at time of war, anyone who with the intention of aiding a hostile power, or of causing harm to the German or allied troops" commits any of the crimes defined in paragraph 90 of the German Penal Code "shall be punished with death for war treason". Specifically, Cavell was charged under paragraph 90 no. 3 Reichsstrafgesetzbuch, for "conveying troops to the enemy", a crime normally punishable by life imprisonment in peacetime.

It was possible to charge Cavell with war treason as paragraph 160 of the German Military Code extended application of paragraph 58 to foreigners "present in the zone of war.

The British government could do nothing to help her. Sir Horace Rowland of the Foreign Office said, "I am afraid that it is likely to go hard with Miss Cavell; I am afraid we are powerless. Lord Robert Cecil, Under-Secretary for Foreign Affairs, advised that, "Any representation by us will do her more harm than good." The United States, however, had not yet joined the war and was able to apply diplomatic pressure. Hugh S. Gibson, First Secretary of the U.S. legation at Brussels, made clear to the German government that executing Cavell would further harm Germany's already damaged reputation.

The German court however started more fires by remarks made by Count Harrach who broke in at this with the rather irrelevant remark that he 'would rather see Miss Cavell' shot than have harm come to the humblest German soldier, and his only regret was that they had not "three or four old English women to shoot." This remark was soon highlighted back at Count Harrach with the words stating, 'may we remind the German civil governor Baron von der Lancken of the burning of Louvain and the sinking of the Lusitania' and told him that this murder of innocent lives would rank with those two affairs and would stir all civilised countries with horror and disgust.

This did not harass Count Harrach he simply gave the order; Of the twenty-seven defendants, five were condemned to death: Cavell, Baucq (an architect in his thirties), Louise Thuliez, Séverin and Countess Jeanne de Belleville. Of the five sentenced to death, but of this decision, only two would be put to death and they would be Cavell and Baucq.

The night before her execution, she told the Reverend H Stirling Gahan, the Anglican chaplain of Christ Church Brussels and former member of staff at Monkton Combe School who had been allowed to see her and to give her Holy Communion, "I am thankful to have had these ten weeks of quiet to get ready. Now I have had them and have been kindly treated here. I expected my sentence and I believe it was just. Standing as I do in view of God and Eternity, I realise that patriotism is not enough, I must have no hatred or bitterness towards anyone."

On 11 October, Baron von der Lancken allowed the execution to proceed. Sixteen men, forming two firing squads, carried out the sentence pronounced on her and on four Belgian men at the National shooting range in Schaerbeek, at 7:00 am on 12 October 1915. There are conflicting reports of the details of Cavell's execution. It states in which she fainted and fell because of her refusal to wear a blindfold in front of the firing squad and Allegedly, while she lay unconscious, a German commanding officer shot her dead with a revolver.

Her execution was represented as an act of German barbarism and moral depravity. The German Secretary for Foreign Affairs made a statement to the press on behalf of the German government: It was a pity that Miss Cavell had to be executed, but it was necessary. She was judged justly ... It is undoubtedly a terrible thing that the woman has been executed; but consider what would happen to a State, particularly in war, if it left crimes aimed at the safety of its armies to go unpunished because they were committed by women.

Yet from personal first-hand experiences of the Red Cross nurse. Pastor Le Saur, the German army chaplain, recalled at the time of her execution, "I do not believe that Miss Cavell wanted to be a martyr ... but she was ready to die for her country ... Miss Cavell was a very brave woman and a faithful Christian". Another account from Anglican chaplain, the Reverend Gahan, remembers Cavell's words, "I have no fear or shrinking; I have seen death so often it is not strange, or fearful to me!"

Edith Cavell's remains were returned to Britain after the war, sailing from Ostend aboard the destroyer HMS Rowena and landing at Admiralty Pier in Dover on 14 May 1919. Edith Cavell was one of only three sets of British remains repatriated following the end of the War, the others being Charles Fryatt and The Unknown Warrior.

 As the ship arrived a full peal of Grandsire Triples (5040 Changes, Parker's Twelve-Part) was rung on the bells of St Mary's Church in the town. A plaque commemorating the peal in the church's bell-ringing chamber states it was "Rung with the bells deeply muffled except for the Tenor, which was open at backstroke, in token of respect to Nurse Cavell.

Her body was transferred to a railway van and lay in state on the Pier overnight before departing from Dover Harbour Station for London Victoria. Becoming known as the Cavell Van, that van is kept as a memorial on the Kent and East Sussex Railway and is usually open to view at Bodiam railway station, though during October 2015 it was placed on display outside the Forum, Norwich.

 From Victoria, the body was processed to Westminster Abbey for a state funeral on 15 May, before finally being reburied at the east side of Norwich Cathedral on 19 May, where a graveside service is still held each October. The brave Norfolk girl was home, a nurse, her execution received worldwide condemnation, she was 49 at the time of her execution, and was already notable as a pioneer of modern nursing in Belgium. A True Norfolk Hero.

https://www.google.com/url?
sa=i&url=http%3A%2F%2Fmaidstonetyphoidepidemic.weebly.com%2Fbiographies-of-
recipients.html&psig=AOvVaw29OCvtBZ10BnbXwhevH66t&ust=1635676821230000&source=im
ages&cd=vfe&ved=2ahUKEwiF5riQ-fHzAhUEhXMKHRIhBdUQr4kDegUIARDPAQ

THE END

General Bibliography

This isn't the bibliography of such when I do my books, but the photos come from the people themselves and it is to these that I thank, the beautiful sunset photos come my photographer friend Malcolm Moulden, the Wherry photograph from Paul Sergeant, the Hay shot from my dear friend Linda Lister. Within the pages of Norfolk Mardling I thank FOND and the writerKeith Skipper of Come Yew tergether. On the thanks side again I acknowledge my associate Tony brooks who designed this prestigious cover and Fakenham prepress for printing such. Pets memories was put in because of friends losing their fur babies and so rightly need acknowledgement… With Chapter Eight Evacuee Alfie comes home I thank Keith Turner for allowing this story to be told, this heart warming tale comes from many on https://wroxhamhistory.wordpress.com I also thank the advertisers for allowing their trade to be mentioned. The Bull in Walsingham, Ramblers of Thurne,Thurne Dynamic Press of Norwich, North Norfolk Embroidery Fakenham, Adam Woodhouse for the upkeep of my website http://www.jdbooklets.org.uk and the help of Esther Fifield of the MNDA for guidance on my just giving page.

Pets Memories

Just this side of heaven is a place called Rainbow Bridge.
When an animal dies that has been especially close to someone here,
that pet goes to Rainbow Bridge. There are meadows and hills for all
of our special friends so they can run and play together. There is plenty
of food, water and sunshine, and our friends are warm and
comfortable.
All the animals who had been ill and old are restored to health and
vigor. Those who were hurt or maimed are made whole and strong
again, just as we remember them in our dreams of days and times
gone by. The animals are happy and content, except for one small
thing; they each miss someone very special to them, who had to be left
behind.
They all run and play together, but the day comes when one suddenly
stops and looks into the distance. His bright eyes are intent. His eager
body quivers. Suddenly he begins to run from the group, flying over the
green grass, his legs carrying him faster and faster.
You have been spotted, and when you and your special friend finally
meet, you cling together in joyous reunion, never to be parted again.
The happy kisses rain upon your face; your hands again caress the
beloved head, and you look once more into the trusting eyes of your
pet, so long gone from your life but never absent from your heart.
Then you cross Rainbow Bridge together....

This page is dedicated to three friends whom have lost their beloved pets since I have
been writing my Norfolk Books.

My Associate Mr Tony Brooks and family who lost their beloved pet 'Custard'.
My dear friend Mr John Hincliffee and family lost ' Bella'
A new customer Marie Martins who was devistated when she lost her pet ' Paddy'

R.I.P. Angels